The Five Fold Ministry:

☐ TRUE

OR

☐ FALSE?

Susan Pryor

The Five Fold Ministry: True or False

by Susan Pryor

ISBN:978-1-935018-68-1

Interior design: Leo Ward
Cover design: Brandon Johnson
Editors: Mary Pratt and Megan Tasdeler

PUBLISHED BY:
Five Stones Publishing
A DIVISION OF:
The International Localization Network
randy2905@gmail.com
ILNcenter.com

DEDICATION

And we beseech you, brethren to know them which labour among you, and are over you in the Lord, and admonish you....

1 Thessalonians 5:12 (NKJV)

Table of Contents

INTRODUCTION

The Bible tells us that Jesus Christ is the Son of God and the Son of Man. It states that He humbled Himself to become a man and that He dwelt among His people (*Philippians 2:5-7*). While on earth, in total submission to the will of His Father, He did the work He was sent to do. In the ultimate example of submission, He who is Life laid down His life and died in order that man, who was dead, might live. Then He arose from the dead and, in great triumph, ascended to His Father in heaven.

While Jesus was on the earth, He laid the foundation for His Church as He helped people to understand that He was—and is—the Christ, the Son of the living God (*Matthew 16:15-18*). Jesus also commissioned saints, both men and women, to preach and publish the good news (the gospel) to every creature of the whole human race (*Mark 16:15*). While the saints were responsible to spread His Word, they were to do so from the context of His Church.

To empower the saints to do as they had been commanded and to enable them to be His witnesses in Jerusalem, Judea, Samaria, and even, in ever widening circles of influence, to the very ends of the earth, He sent His Holy Spirit to baptize them in efficiency and might *(Acts 1:8)*.

Further, to enable the Church to function as one godly, holy body, He gave gifts to it. These ascension gifts were very specific: *"When He ascended on high, He led captivity captive, and gave gifts to men. And He Himself gave some to be apostles, some prophets, some evangelists, and some pastors and teachers" (Ephesians 4:11 NKJV)*.

Please note that these gifts were not presents wrapped in pretty paper and bows. Rather, they were and are men and women of God. They are saints who Jesus has divinely appointed to represent Him on earth as He manifests specific functions or facets of His priesthood through them. The gifts of apostles, prophets, evangelists, pastors and teachers were bestowed, brought forth, made or set in place in the Church to equip and perfect the saints for the work of ministry and to edify His body. These gifts were also to be a safeguard, keeping saints from the error of false doctrine and from the deceptions of unscrupulous men *(Ephesians 4:12-14)*.

Perhaps a short comparison is in order. As will be seen, in upcoming chapters, the working of holy gifts will be labeled in three ways:

- First is the **grace** or initial nudging of a gift. It is the introduction or slow entry into the realm of the supernatural in a particular area of God's blessings. When a gift such as those listed in 1 Corinthians 12 is given, it may take the recipient of the gift time to realize that the things he is thinking or she feels like doing (such as walking in a greater measure of faith, healing the sick) are really the call or instruction by God to begin to do so.

- Second is the **ministry** or on-going operation of a spiritual gift by a member of the body of Christ. When one who has received grace to operate in one or more of the above mentioned spiritual gifts has faithfully done so to the point that that his or her work is recognized by the leadership of the local Church as valid, that saint's spiritual gifts now become a recognized ministry.

- Third are the **gifts given as Jesus rose on high** as listed in *Ephesians 4.*

The first two, the grace and the ministry, are gifts of the Holy Spirit. They function primarily on a horizontal level in local churches and communities and are the expression of the Holy Spirit ministering to people for the common good. Such gifts would include words of wisdom, words of knowledge, faith, healing, working miracles, prophecy, discerning spirits, tongues, and interpreting tongues *(1 Corinthians 12:7-10).*

The third are gifts of Jesus. They operate on a vertical level at both the local and universal Church levels and are the expression of God's Word, will, and way *through* those He has raised up to be apostles, prophets, evangelists, pastors, and teachers.

These last gifts, because they were given when Jesus ascended on high, are sometimes called ascension gifts.

Some deny their importance or even their existence and say they are not relevant in today's Church. Nothing could be further from the truth. Without these gifts and honorable saints walking in them, there is no true Church. Furthermore, *Romans 11:29* clearly states that the gifts and callings of God are irrevocable.

One argument against the validity of these gifts declares that with the death of the first century apostles and prophets these gifts or callings died out too. This erroneous doctrine of man is not supported by Scripture. Nowhere does the Bible, which clearly describes the giving of these gifts, state that God recalled them. While it is very true that the bodies of the saints who years ago graced these gifts or Church offices died, the gifts themselves did not. The gifts are spiritual not physical. They are therefore eternal in nature, not temporal. They did not and cannot die.

Continuing the argument against the ascension gifts, some assert that Scripture does not teach the doctrine of apostolic succession. They then conclude that because there is no legitimate apostolic succession in the way that man now practices it, there is no apostolic office.

It is quite true that today's apostles are not authorized to raise up apostles or to lay their mantle of authority on others of *their own choosing*. Therefore, objections to this, the modern practice of apostolic succession, are well founded. However, it is also true that God in His sovereignty does have the right to raise up apostles and to give them the authority to act in His name. As shown in Acts 13:1-3, it was God who chose the first apostles and He who raised up their successors so that His work would continue.

A third area of discussion maintains that while the offices of apostle and prophet are obsolete, the last three, those of evangelist, pastor, and teacher, are not. This idea is not logical. If God had withdrawn some of His offices, would He not have withdrawn all of them? As we will soon learn, apostles and prophets are to build and direct God's Church. The other three offices fill it, care for it, and teach it. In God's true Church there would be nothing to fill and no one to keep or instruct if the apostles and prophets were not doing their jobs.

A final argument against the ascension gifts is that these offices are irrelevant in today's Church. Are they? God gave the offices to equip the saints for the work of ministry (Ephesians 4:11-12). Are saints fully equipped? Do they or do just their leaders minister? He gave the gifts to build the body of Christ. Is it edified? He gave the gifts until there is a unity of faith, a knowledge of Christ, and a maturity in the saints. Is there unity in Him? Is the Church knowledgeable? Is it mature?

If the answer to any these questions is no, then the work of the ascension gifts and those who are called to them isn't yet finished. If the gifts were given until a certain result was realized and that goal has not yet been reached, then the Church needs gifted saints working in these positions until the work is accomplished.

The ascension gifts were not given while Jesus was here just to get the Church through its birthing and childhood. They were given to allow the Church to carry out His business and to do His work until His return. If God has assigned the Church the task of spreading the gospel throughout the world and given His gifts and offices as the means to complete that task, He wouldn't just capriciously remove that means before the job was finished. His ascension gifts are in effect on earth until the work of the Church is done.

We must remember that God declared that He would build a Church (*Matthew 16:18*) from which the Word would go forth. Surely He would do nothing to hinder the intent of His heart. The Church may not as yet have fulfilled its assigned function, but the fault does not lie with God. Rather, the Church must acknowledge that it has been deceived by the enemy into thinking God's gifts were either recalled or irrelevant. It must place the blame for this error squarely on its own shoulders. It must repent of the fact that it has allowed itself to be deceived, manipulated, and cheated in the outworking of His gifts by many ruthless, ungodly men who rendered those gifts almost useless through confusion and error.

There are many claiming to be in the body of Christ who did not come in by way of the cross of Christ. They neither know nor follow the Word and have never truly repented or confessed their sins. Nor have they sacrificed self. These, while they know not God's ways, yet seek His means. They want His power to do as He did, but they refuse to be as He is: holy.

There are among us today many contenders for God's throne but few for His altar. Many who are not willing to pay the price of service, the denial of self, take short cuts to power. They seek show, public acclaim, the manifestation of miracles, gifts, and offices at no cost to self. This is not to imply that God's gifts can be bought or earned, for their price is free. But the cost is high: we must give up self.

While many are truly called of God, serve Him well, and accomplish wonders in His name and with His blessing, there are also many arising who are unwilling to go through the Lord's school of discipleship, meet His standards, or follow His way. Since they want a ministry so badly, they slap a label on themselves (or convince the undiscerning to do it for them) and begin to walk in their own way. They entitle themselves with whatever they decide they want to be and begin to carnally act out their unwise, unanointed version of that office. In the process, they trick, deceive, and mislead the saints.

In spite of any claim or effort to the contrary, if a work is not ordained by God, empowered by Him, and dedicated to His service, it is not His. Much trouble, confusion, and error permeate the body of Christ today because of the acts, the pretense, the deception, and the counterfeiting of the true ministries of God by unscrupulous men and women.

It is the purpose of this book to bring the true Church into an awareness of the ascension gifts of the Lord. It is to describe each gift and to profile the persons with that gift. It is not intended to be a tome of infinite detail but a simple, basic guide aspiring to briefly present some of the marks of the true gift and truly gifted and then to expose the false or counterfeit minister and ministry. It will contrast true with false, godly with ungodly, holy with evil.

To those who want to argue that there are four gifts rather than five, for the purposes of this writing, please understand that since five offices are listed in *Ephesians 4:11*, five will be discussed. Whether the Word should read pastor-teacher or pastor and teacher is outside the scope of this book. While elders or pastors must be able to teach (*"Feed My sheep" John 21:17*), it is not a requirement that all teachers be elders. Therefore, with that distinction, this writing recognizes each position as a separate office or gift and treats each in separate chapters.

Additionally, I want to make it clear that women as well as men are given the ministries of apostle, prophet, evangelist, pastor, and teacher. Throughout the remainder of this book, I will use only the pronoun "he" when I am discussing the five-fold ministers. This is only for simplicity and is not in any way meant to imply that women are excluded from these positions. Therefore, as you continue reading, feel free to mentally substitute the word "she" for "he" if you wish.

A final desire in the undertaking is to entreat Christians to pray for the revival of the godly five-fold ministry and to understand the earnest need of discernment.

Christians everywhere now more than ever need the boldness to believe and to walk in His calling and the ability to judge spirits in order to throw off the darkness of deception and to walk in His marvelous light.

APOSTLES: THE TRUE

"And He Himself gave some to be apostles"
Ephesians 4:11 (NKJV)

As listed in *Ephesians 4:11*, the first in the list of blessings that Jesus gave to the Church is the apostle. Every work must have a beginning. In the Church, starting things or laying the foundation is the work of an apostle.

The English word apostle and its meaning "to send from" come from a combination of Greek words: the verb *stello*, which means "to send," and the preposition *apo*, which means "from." An apostle is one who is sent forth from the Church.

GOOD CHARACTER

Before looking more closely at what an apostle does, it is wise to learn who he is.

A TRUE APOSTLE IS HOLY: In character, an apostle must be holy (*Ephesians 3:5*). That is, he must be devout, separated, set aside, and wholly dedicated to God. An apostle is honest, righteous, fair, and a person known to be trustworthy. Honor and goodness mark his character.

He must also be a person of impeccable conduct. He is strong, stable, and virtuous.

A TRUE APOSTLE IS A PERSON OF INTEGRITY: Since he is integrated with, or one with God, he desires to bring others into unity, cohesion, and oneness with Him too. He longs to bring the parts of the true Church together to make a whole.

An apostle's character is marked by integrity and submission.

A TRUE APOSTLE IS UNDER AUTHORITY: An apostle is submitted to God. He is a person who recognizes and acknowledges that he is not his own. Though some may look upon the apostle as one being at the top of the list of Church leadership and think that he who labors from this lofty position has no one to be accountable to, an apostle is still fully and at all times accountable both to God and to people. He can only effectively minister when he is submitted to the Word, will, and ways of God and in holy relationship serving God's people.

A TRUE APOSTLE WALKS IN AUTHORITY: In addition to holiness, integrity, and submission, an apostle is a person whose hallmark is authority. Since he is under authority to God, he is given great authority by God to accomplish what he is asked to do. As one called by God and sent out by the Church, he is supernaturally endowed with spiritual blessing. He carries the anointing and authority of God as he

An apostle's ministry is marked by authority and perseverance.

extends the kingdom of God on earth. His ministry is often accompanied by signs, none of which bring glory to him but all of which glorify the One who sent him.

A TRUE APOSTLE ENDURES: An apostle is a person of perseverance (2 *Corinthians* 12:12). Paul's descriptions in 2 *Corinthians* 11:25-27 of the hardships he suffered while serving the Lord make it easy to see that the gift of apostle is no easy task. It is not for the faint of heart.

It is of the utmost importance that an apostle be the right person for the work. He must be able to endure hardship and rejection. He must meet the requirements for the position of elder since he is often considered a co-elder or co-leader in a local Church (1 *Timothy* 3:1-7).

WHAT DOES AN APOSTLE DO?

What then is this one who is sent forth to do? What is his mission?

A TRUE APOSTLE ESTABLISHES THE CHURCH: The *New Strong's Exhaustive Concordance of the Bible* declares that an apostle is "a delegate, a commissioner of Christ, and an ambassador of the gospel." *The Amplified Bible* adds that an apostle is a special messenger. And so He is! An apostle is a person of vision who sees God's purpose (*Acts* 22:17-21) and sets about accomplishing it. Specifically, he establishes God's Church; he builds the dwelling place of God on earth. In so doing, he extends the kingdom of God on earth.

This Church is not a denomination or a building of wood, brick, or stone; it is the body of Christ. In building the Church, an apostle is a pioneer. It is his job to go before the main body and establish a base so that those who follow will have something on which to build. An apostle spiritually and physically precedes others into an area. This area can include expansion into geographical areas that do not know Christ or Christianity and from which the Church, one established, can introduce the good news of salvation. It can also include the spreading the gospel and introducing Christianity into the areas of finance, commerce, banking, medicine, education, science, religions, entertainment, and the arts. In this way, the *"kingdoms of this world....become the kingdoms of our Lord and of His Christ" (Revelations 11:15 NKJV).*

An apostle is charged to lay the Church's substructure in Christ *(Ephesians 2:19-22).* In the world, when something needs to be built, there must be both those able to do the physical work and a leader to oversee the construction. This headman or foreman has authority over the workers and over the project. He is the one in charge. He is responsible for preparing the way, laying the foundation, and administrating the building of the project. With a crew, he has a job to do.

Similarly, in order to build the Church there must be a construction crew under the leadership of a boss or overseer. The work crew is made up of saints while the foreman, the one with the authority for the project, is the apostle. Together they are commissioned to build the kingdom of God on earth.

An apostle is often a composite of other gifts. If necessary he must be a "man for all seasons," able and ready to do any and all jobs that he requires of his workers. He can therefore function in any job if the need arises. He must supervise every phase of the building process. Unlike those who labor over buildings of metal, glass, and stone, the apostle does his utmost to raise a spiritual structure of faith, obedience, and love, the temple of God.

When the foundation, Jesus Christ, is properly laid, the apostle must oversee the building of the infrastructure and the raising of the walls. Praise, worship, and prayer must be the flooring of the Church; righteousness, truth, justice, honor, goodness, forgiveness, and love must be the very fabric of its walls; mercy must roof it or be the cover over all.

Hear Paul as he describes his work as an apostle: *"According to the grace of God which was given to me, as a wise master builder I have laid the foundation…."* (*1 Corinthians 3:10 NKJV*).

A TRUE APOSTLE DECLARES DOCTRINE: An apostle declares Church doctrine (*Acts 2:42*). If a foundation is laid wrong, that which is built upon it will never be right. If the base is askew or weak, so is the building. Spiritually speaking, if the Church is not built according to His plan, it is not God's Church.

To prevent such difficulties or setbacks from happening to His Church, God left believers with a design or prototype. Holy Scripture lays out His plan. The blueprint of the Church is the Word of God. Any structure of His must be built according to His plan and His Word.

Each foundation stone of the Church is an authoritative declaration of true biblical doctrine. In their expounding on God's Word, apostles must be very careful. No human is charged with telling God what His Word "really" means. No human is charged with changing the Word to emphasize or authenticate the doctrines of men. No human should add to the Word; any revelation should not be a new Word or an addition to the Word but should only be a new insight or biblically verifiable understanding of the already complete and wholly true written Word of God. Similarly, no human should subtract from the Word, omitting vital parts of it. An apostle is simply charged to declare the whole Word of God—no more, no less.

An apostle lays the foundation for, declares doctrine for, and governs the Church.

A TRUE APOSTLE GOVERNS: In addition to building the Church, an apostle is charged to oversee the government of the Church. As the apostle Paul did, an apostle sets in place those who will lead the Church *(Acts 14:23)*. And, as the apostle Paul did, he disciplines it *(1 Corinthians 5:1-5)*. When he sees wrong, it is his job to make it right.

Putting all of this together, it is the apostle's job to see that the Church is laid on a sure foundation. Paul informs us: *"Now, therefore, you are no longer strangers and foreigners, but fellow citizens with the saints and members of the household of God having been built on the foundation of the apostles and prophets.... "* (Ephesians 2:19-20 NKJV).

The sure foundation he lays is Jesus Christ. *"For no other foundation can anyone lay than that which is laid, Jesus Christ"* (1 Corinthians 3:11 NKJV).

There comes a time after the foundation is laid and the structure is sound when the work of the apostle is finished in that place. An apostle of God knows when his work is done and it is time to leave. A true apostle must be aware that there is no such thing as founding a work and then camping on it forever. It never becomes his. Often an apostle will birth a baby (metaphorically speaking) and then be asked by God to move on to another work long before he sees the baby fully grown or matured.

GOD'S AMBASSADOR

Agreeing with *The New Strong's Exhaustive Concordance of the Bible*, it can clearly be seen that an apostle is like an ambassador.

An ambassador is one sent out from a particular country or government. As such he represents that country, has the authority of that government invested in him, and acts on its behalf by standing in for the leader of that country.

> **An apostle acts as God's ambassador.**

Similarly, an apostle, God's holy ambassador, has been appointed by God and sent out to represent Him on earth. He has the authority of God's government invested

23

in him. He acts on behalf of or stands in for the Head of that kingdom, Jesus Christ. It is only after acknowledging that God, not he, has the true authority and power that he is able to represent God on earth.

He is totally submitted to God in the area assigned to him. Mark well! In arrogance he does not represent himself to the Church or to the world. By coercion or tradition he doesn't represent institutional religion to the Church and to the world. Rather, he is so one with the Father that there is no thought of or presentation of his own goals or ambitions. In humbleness and faith, he simply represents God to the Church and to the world. He has been given God's authority (*Luke 10:19*) and he must use it by acting on God's behalf.

LEVELS OF APOSTLES

It is from the local Church that those who minister in the universal Church spring forth. At the local level there are at least three levels of anointing: the grace, the ministry gift, and the full fledged anointing on one who serves in the five–fold ministry. Faithfulness in each of these leads to promotion in the local Church. Only God can call His saints to a five-fold ministry across greater geographical areas.

Concerning the apostle, there can be seen in a local Church some with the call of apostleship on their lives.

THE GRACE OF APOSTLE: Those with the grace of apostleship begin to recognize and to follow their call in service to God in the local Church. They are people of vision who delight in pioneering new projects and then, once the projects are well established, in turning them over to able administrators. Those with the grace of apostle love being in on the beginning of a project and laying its foundations.

THE MINISTRY OF APOSTLE: Those with the ministry gift of apostle expand their parameters to a larger field. They are willing to go out and do the unusual. In their love to initiate a work, they are often involved in church planting projects. They honorably exercise the authority given them and represent their God and His Church well in their community. They find that they can easily adapt to foreign lands and cultures and so are often involved in missionary efforts. As they grow in ministry, they preach and teach with authority and signs and wonders may begin to be seen.

THE APOSTLE: A duly appointed and anointed apostle serves in his local Church but is then sent out to do the work of God in a larger arena. Some go to foreign fields to lay the foundation of the Church from which the will of God can be done *"on earth as it is in heaven."* Others are pioneers of the gospel and of God's Word, will, and ways in the fields of medicine, finance, or education. Wherever he is sent, it is always the primary objective of an apostle to represent God and establish His kingdom.

HOW ARE APOSTLES CHOSEN?

An apostle is neither a self-made nor man-made man. His calling is from God alone. *"Paul, an apostle (not from men* nor through man, but through Jesus Christ and God the Father who raised Him from the dead)" *(Galatians 1:1 NKJV).*

True apostleship is by appointment of God only. It originated with God who sent out His Son, Jesus *(John 3:16).* When ministering on earth, Jesus, in turn, called twelve disciples to Himself *(Matthew 10:1),* gave them authority for a mission, and sent them out as apostles *(Matthew 10:2).* Later, after His resurrection but before His ascension, Jesus again sent out disciples: *"As the Father has sent Me, I also send you" (John 20:21 NKJV).* When He returned to heaven, Jesus gave the gift of apostle to the Church *(Ephesians 4:11).*

In the first century Peter declared that only those who had seen Jesus and who had been witnesses of His ministry were qualified to be apostles. However, by raising up Paul, who did not fit Peter's (or man's) requirements, God demonstrated that He could pick anyone He so chose by His sovereign grace.

Apostles are appointed by God alone.

That pattern continues today. At some point in his life, through revelation of the Holy Spirit, a fledgling apostle recognizes God's call in his life. In successfully submitting to God for training and discipline, his calling and gifts are recognized by the leaders and elders of God's Church. In God's time, he is identified as an apostle, commissioned and sent out. He does what he has been asked to do, and returns to his local Church.

Since God does the raising and the Church does the sending, it should be quite apparent that there is no such thing as apostolic succession. No one has either the privilege of designating himself an apostle or the right to raise others into that job. He is not authorized to leave his position as a legacy to another of his own choosing. Apostles do not beget apostles. Only God does!

JESUS, THE APOSTLE

If saints are to really agree on the validity of the office of apostle in today's Church, they should seek truth concerning it in the Word. Does Scripture approve of apostles or prohibit them? Does it endorse them or deny them?

The Word identifies Jesus as an apostle: *"Therefore, holy brethren, partakers of the holy calling, consider the Apostle and High Priest of our confession, Christ Jesus...."* *(Hebrews 3:1 NKJV).*

As an apostle, Jesus is the perfection of that office. At the beginning of His apostleship on earth, He was sent out from heaven by His Father *(John 5:24,30)*. While here on earth, He acted **Jesus is the** as His Father's ambassador, used His au- **Apostle of** thority, preached His Word, and laid the **apostles.** foundation of His Church. He corrected erroneous doctrine when men tried to superimpose their ways, beliefs, and traditions over the true way *(Matthew 15)*. His earthly apostleship wonderfully evidenced signs, wonders, and miracles. After Jesus had done all He was asked to do, He ascended to heaven, returning to the One who had sent Him. He did all this in absolute selflessness, holiness, and submission, an Apostle of highest character.

FIRST CENTURY APOSTLES

While on earth, Jesus called together a group of disciples. He taught them and trained them. Then from their ranks He chose some whom He equipped and sent out to do specific works *(Luke 9:1-2)*. When they returned to report to Him, they were no longer referred to as disciples but as apostles *(Matthew 10:2; Luke 9:10)*.

Since Jesus chose, trained, authorized, and commissioned these apostles to go out on His behalf, it would be appropriate to ascertain the reason for their calling or to learn what they were sent out to do. In short, did they use Jesus as a role model and do as He did, or did they use His name and authority to do their own thing?

These first century apostles were truly ambassadors for the Lord. They used His authority to do what He sent them out to do. They had received what must have seemed to them a unique commission. They were given authority and power over demons and diseases and told by Jesus to preach and to heal the sick *(Luke 9:1-2)*. Additionally, the gospel of Matthew reveals that the fledgling apostles were to cleanse lepers, raise the dead, and cast out demons *(Matthew 10:7-8)*.

Later, Jesus sent out seventy others who were also told to preach that the kingdom of God was near and to heal the sick *(Luke 10:1,9)*. When they returned, they had discovered that the authority of Jesus' name caused even demons to be subject to them *(Luke 10:17)*.

When Jesus finished His earthly ministry, rose from the dead, and ascended into heaven, He gave gifts to the saints (*Ephesians 4:8*) to edify and build up the body of Christ, the Church, that He had founded on the Rock. In other words, Jesus not only authorized saints to preach the Word, but He told them, by means of His gifts, to build a Church to use as a base of operations for so doing. Jesus did not take away ministry offices in the first century. Instead, He gave them to saints for the specific purpose of building His Church for use as a launching pad for worldwide evangelism.

All of this, while wonderful, is yet a cause for concern. Jesus was a perfect man, and He could perfectly execute the office of apostle. However, was it possible for His believers or first century saints of God to walk in all that this office entails?

The answer was a resounding yes. To show us that people can do it, in His Word, God teaches us in His Word that people have already done it.

For example, Peter was a man called by God to be an **Peter was sent as an apostle to the Jews.** apostle to the Jews. As such, he compellingly preached the Word (*Acts 2*) and signs and wonders accompanied his ministry (*Acts 3:1-6*). He corrected erroneous doctrine (*Acts 15*), and as a result of his obedience, a strong Church was built in Jerusalem (*Acts 3:7*). Though in worldly eyes a poor fisherman and though he had no Bible schooling or theological degrees under his belt, he admirably fulfilled his calling as an apostle.

Paul, too, was an early apostle in the Church who was sent out to minister to the Gentiles. Paul, who had not been an eye-witness of the life and ministry of Christ nor a member of His inner circle as Peter had been, was yet a powerful apostle. After his conversion on the Damascus Road, Paul went away for some time. While gone, he learned about and heard from God. God revealed Himself to Paul.

Paul was sent as an apostle to the Gentiles.

> For this reason I, Paul, the prisoner of Jesus Christ for you Gentiles—if indeed you have heard of the dispensation of the grace of God which was given to me for you, how that by revelation He made known to me the mystery (as I wrote before in a few words, by which, when you read, you may understand my knowledge in the mystery of Christ), which in other ages was not made known to the sons of men, as it has now been revealed by the Spirit to His holy apostles and prophets....Ephesians 3:1-5 (NKJV)

Paul became a servant of Christ and a steward of the mysteries of God (*1 Corinthians 4:1*). As a saint, he preached (*Ephesians 3:8*), corrected error (*1 Corinthians 4:21*), and taught the Word (*1 Corinthians 4:17*). His epistles are recognized even today as foundational Church doctrine and comprise thirteen books of the New Testament.

Some who were prophets in the Church at Antioch, while fasting and praying, had the Holy Spirit reveal to them that Paul was to be separated out and sent forth for a special work. After further fasting and praying and laying on of hands, Paul was indeed sent out to preach the Word and lay the foundation of Christ and build the Church *(Acts 13:1-3)*. He did not lay this foundation where others had already begun building; instead he went where others had not gone before *(2 Corinthians 10:13-15)*. Paul further describes his ministry as follows:

> For we are God's fellow workers; you are God's field, you are God's building. According to the grace of God which was given to me, **as a wise master builder I have laid the foundation,** and another builds on it. But let each one take heed how he builds on it. For no other foundation can anyone lay than that which is laid, which is Jesus Christ. *[emphasis added]* 1 Corinthians 3:9-11(NKJV)

As an apostle, Paul realized that his job was to begin a work but not necessarily to stay long enough to see it fully completed. He said, *"I planted, Apollos watered, but God gave the increase"* *(1 Corinthians 3:6)*.

When Paul finished a work in a designated area, when a Church was begun, trained, and matured enough to carry on God's work, he turned the work over to those raised up as leaders *(Acts 14:21-23)* and moved to another area. Several times he returned to Antioch to report to the brethren who had sent him out (Acts 14:26-28; 15:30-35; 18:18-22).

Further, Paul realized that his work had to face the test of fire. Both his adherence to the true Word and his building of

God's Church had to face the tests of authenticity and eternity. He knew that the false and the temporal, or the hay and the stubble, would be burned (1 Corinthians 3:11-15). For instance, when members of the Church in Corinth went into moral error it was Paul who stepped in with correction and discipline (1 Corinthians 5:1-6). When the churches in Galatia went into doctrinal error it was Paul who stepped in to denounce the gospel of law and works and to defend the gospel of faith (Galatians 1-5). In so doing, he gave direction and re-laid the foundation of true Church doctrine.

TWENTY-FIRST CENTURY APOSTLES

Though Peter and Paul both easily pass the tests of apostleship, what about other people? What about saints in the Church today?

Before He left earth, Jesus spoke forth that which has become known as the Great Commission. He said to His disciples:

> All authority has been given to Me in heaven and on earth. Go therefore and make disciples of all the nations, baptizing them in the name of the Father and of the Son and of the Holy Spirit, teaching them to observe all things that I have commanded you; and lo, I am with you always, even to the end of the age. Matthew 18:18-20 (NKJV)

> Go into all the world and preach the gospel to every creature. Mark 16:15 (NKJV)

> *Thus it is written, and thus it was necessary for the Christ to suffer and to rise from the dead the third day, and that repentance and remission of sins should be preached in His name to all nations, beginning at Jerusalem. Luke 24:46 (NKJV)*

Jesus came to earth and, as an apostle, trained men into that position, showed that people could function in that calling, and commissioned the saints to go forth to preach the gospel to the end of the world (both in time and place). This commission is valid until the job is done.

God has given apostles to the 21st century Church. Further, Jesus gave gifts to build up the Church from which to send forth the Word and the workers of the Word. Since these have been continuously needed and utilized for over 2,000 years, clearly the gift of apostle is not only valid but is as essential in the twenty-first century as it was in the first.

A FINAL NOTE

As a final note concerning true apostles, the Word says,

"For I think that God has displayed us, the apostles, last...." (1 Corinthians 4:9 NKJV).

How true is His Word!

When Israel regained her homeland in 1948, God's time clock seemed to start its final countdown. In the 1950s, God sent wonderful, gifted evangelists into a dark world to preach the Word and millions of the lost came to know Jesus as Savior. In the 1960s, the Lord raised up gifted pastors to care for His increasing flock. The 1970s saw the rise of talented teachers who instructed the saints about their Lord. The 1980s and 1990s witnessed a dramatic explosion in the prophetic ministry. That leaves, in this new century and in this age of grace, one ministry to go.

The apostles are truly to be displayed last. God is readying an army willing to go out to reach the farthest corners of the earth with His good news. He's building His Church, and as soon as His bride is ready, she will join her Groom. Today, the time of the rising apostolic ministry, will see the Church maturing and coming into a spiritual unity as she grows up unto her Head, Christ *(Ephesians 4:15).*

This will not be a false unity founded on the spurious agreements among religious leaders who would countenance and conceal biblical error rather than to confront and expose it in order to preserve the ambitious ministries of men. Nor will it be a false unity based on the doctrines, denominations, and traditions of men. It will be unity with and in God.

When the Word has gone forth by the work of true apostles and the bride is complete, then she and her Groom will be one.

A COMPARISON

	The Grace	The Ministry	The Apostle
Reference:	Matthew 10:1,5 Luke 9:1-2	Matther 10:1.5 Luke 9:1-2	Ephesians 4:11
Source:	Jesus	Jesus	Jesus
For Whom:	all	all	some
Where:	local Church	local Church and community	local Church, community, and the world
When:	when called and commissioned by the local Church	when called and commissioned by the local Church	when called and sent out by the local Church
Purpose:	represent the kingdom of God in the local Church	represent the kingdom of God in the local Church and community	represent God and His kingdom to the local Church, community, and world
Methods:	teach Biblical doctrine and build the local Church	teach Biblical doctrine and engage in church planting in the denomination and in the community	declare Biblical doctrine, lay the foundation and govern the Church, establish the Church in a world-wide setting

APOSTLES: THE FALSE

"For such are false apostles, deceitful workers...."
2 Corinthians 11:13 (NKJV)

In the previous chapter it was mentioned that a sure foundation must be laid in order for a strong structure to be raised. If the base of a building is not strong, deep, and straight, that which is built on top of it will be weak. Built on a tottering, faulty foundation, it will waver, tremble, crumble, and eventually fall. Laying a sure foundation is the work of a true apostle; laying a weak, crumbling foundation is the work of a false one.

It is sad but true that every truth in the Word is opposed by the false or counterfeit. Those in darkness seek to deceive people and lead them away from the light of the truth. While the Bible teaches of godly apostles, it also clearly labels some as false apostles.

Since we now know the description and manner of true apostles, saints must learn to discern false ones. They will exhibit opposite traits, motives, and methods of the true apostles of God. However, since false apostles are masters of deception and of the counterfeit, these differences are not always easy to see.

BAD CHARACTER

As the calling, job, methods, and authority of a true apostle differ completely from those of a false apostle, so too the character of the true apostle differs from that of the false apostle. Rather than being a holy, open, honest minister known for his honor and integrity, the false apostle is a master of deception who beguiles the unwary. He lies and misrepresents himself in order to appear to be what he is not. The Bible describes his personality and character in very strong words:

> For [although] they hold a form of piety (true religion), they deny and reject and are strangers to the power of it—their conduct belies the genuineness of their profession. Avoid [all] such people—turn away from them. For among them are those who worm their way into homes and captivate silly and weak-natured and spiritually dwarfed women, loaded down with [the burdens of their] sins, [and easily] swayed and led away by various evil desires and seductive impulses. [These weak women will listen to anybody who will teach them]; they are forever inquiring and getting information, but are never able to arrive at a recognition and knowledge of the Truth. 2 Timothy 3:5-7 (TAB)

SEDUCTION: A false apostle is a seducer; he is a fraud and a charlatan. Often not recognizing himself as such, he masquerades and postures; he manip-

A false apostle is a seducer.

ulates and dominates. He presents truth as lies and lies as truth. His character matches his message—phony.

REBELLION: In addition to being deceptive, a false apostle is rebellious. A false apostle refuses to see the error of his ways. He will neither repent nor return to God. In fact he has turned the office of apostle around. Rather than presenting a true Word and correcting erroneous doctrine, he himself presents error and stands in need of correction. However, since he is under no authority, he will neither correct others nor allow himself to be corrected. He knows that if he began to correct error he would have to start with himself and in the process he might lose his own little kingdom. Thus, in his stubbornness, he moves even farther away from the main body of truth into even deeper error and finds himself ever more strongly under the control of the false god he represents.

The profile of a false apostle is not a pretty one. Since apostles are the beginners of a work or the layers of a foundation, the Church rises or falls with this ministry. Unfortunately, there are false apostles at work in the body of Christ who are not being identified as such by an unsuspecting, undiscerning Church.

WHAT DOES A FALSE APOSTLE DO?

Just as God's true apostle has a mission to accomplish, so too a false apostle executes a specific task. Therefore, since false apostles are a threat to the true Church, it is wise to inquire what the goals and functions of the counterfeit apostolic ministry are.

THE FIVE FOLD MINISTRY: *True or False?*

A FALSE APOSTLE SPEAKS A FALSE WORD: Since a true apostle is to preach the Word and build the Church, it

A false apostle destroys the Church.

is the intention and the fruit of the false apostle to do just the opposite. A false apostle does not impart God's Word. Rather, he teaches *a* word but not *the* Word. A false apostle does not proclaim the objective Word of God; he entices with a subjective word. Further, a false apostle does not correct erroneous doctrine; instead he introduces it. In other words, he proclaims as unerring fact false doctrine which promotes man or denomination and builds a false church on outright error.

Since Jesus, the Word, was made flesh and since the Word is God *(John 1:1)*, all preaching of the Word should be centered in Him. As Jesus is the Way, the Truth and the Life *(John 14:6)*, no one should say anything contrary to His will or His ways. Ignoring this, a false apostle opposes truth. He often speaks a beguiling message that begins in the Word but ends in the world. He brings humanism and immature expression of emotion or self into his preaching which in effect dilutes the true Word and leads to conformity to man's word.

A FALSE APOSTLE LEADS PEOPLE AWAY FROM GOD: In addition to the error and confusion that he introduces concerning the Word of God, a false apostle does not lay a proper foundation concerning man's relationship with God either. Instead of setting a steady course toward God and leading others to Him, false apostles sail away from

Him, taking all those they have captured with them. By preaching a false word and doctrine and by pulling saints from the truth, they tear down rather than build the true Church.

Then the false one builds a false church. He raises his own group and keeps it separate from God's (Acts 5:37-38). He isolates his flock and continues to feed them poison. Raiding the flock of God, he builds a religion centered around man or Satan. Often this becomes a cult with the false apostle as its leader. Using his false revelation as the cornerstone, he adds error onto error until he has formed a confused hodge-podge that threatens to collapse on itself.

An example of this is a group known as the People's Temple. After a charismatic man named Jim Jones began this group in Indiana in the 1950s, thousands began to follow him. While Jones claimed to be a Christian, in truth his message seemed a dangerous conglomeration of communism, false healing, false teaching, and "us vs. them." Then tragedy struck in 1978 in their compound located in Guyana, Africa. When faced with exposure of truth about his "ministry," Jones ordered his followers to swallow a fruit drink laced with cyanide in a mass suicide-murder. Hundreds died because they believed this false apostle.

LEVELS OF FALSE APOSTLES

1. **TRUE CALLING, WRONG TIMING:** The first false apostle is one who may truly have a calling of God on his life, but his methods and timing, though well intended, are all

wrong. He may really have received a vision or revelation that is without question a part of the working out of God's plan. Or, he may have believed that the call to preach the gospel to all people and make disciples of all nations is his command to go forth now. Not checking his plans with the leaders of his Church to see if he is in error, not waiting for God's direction, timing, or training, with no anointing from God or release from his local body, he goes forth anyway. Unprepared to preach or teach, unable to build, unlearned in the Word, his ignorance and zeal lead to error. Often working alone,

False apostle #1 sees himself as a knight in shining armor but really is a rebellious lone ranger.

he sees himself as a knight in shining armor out to enlighten the masses. In truth, he is a rebellious "lone ranger" bringing trouble wherever he goes. This false apostle has much to learn from the book of Acts concerning the proper calling of an apostle:

> Now in the church that was at Antioch there were certain prophets and teachers: Barnabas, Simeon who was called Niger, Lucius of Cyrene, Manaen who had been brought up with Herod the tetrarch, and Saul. As they ministered to the Lord and fasted, the Holy Spirit said, "Now separate to Me Barnabas and Saul for the work to which I have called them." Acts 13:1-2 (NKJV)

Note that Paul and Barnabas did not announce to the others that they had been called to be apostles. Instead, while Church leaders were gathered together fasting and praying the Holy Spirit informed them that Paul and Barnabas were being called into an apostolic work. However, even with a clear calling from God, the two did not immediately jump up and run off. The next verse continues: *"Then after fasting and praying they put their hands on them and sent them away" (Acts 13:3 TAB).*

Fasting and praying made the saints aware of the call on Paul and Barnabas. It was after further fasting and praying that Paul and Barnabas *were sent out.* Any "apostle" who will not wait for God, any who neglects to be sent out by the saints, any who moves out rebelliously to promote his own works in his own time is a false apostle.

A second lesson that we can learn from these verses is that the apostles were not singly sent out. They went in twos. Following the pattern established by Jesus *(Luke 10:1)* in sending out the apostles two by two, so here two men were commissioned to go out together as apostles. For their protection, for companionship, and to guard against error, the early kingdom builders were sent out in pairs. No lone apostles graced or disgraced God's ministry.

The false apostle would know his work or revelation was in error if he had acted correctly instead of rebelliously. In the kingdom of God, no one is to walk alone. All saints are part of one body and, to function properly, they are interdependent upon one another. Often, a false apostle does not acknowledge this. His "new word" is his own word, not the Word of God. Since he is not truly submitted to a local Church, he will not submit his private revelation to the leaders of that Church for denial or confirmation. The false apostle does not emulate Paul, who traveled to Jerusalem to present his ministry for validation or for correction to the apostles and leaders of that Church and in so doing received their commendation (*Acts 9:27-28; Galatians 2:1-10*). Instead a false apostle becomes so impressed with his own ideas that, rather than being sent off by a local body, he just goes off in rebellion and does what is right in his own eyes.

2. **THE MAN OF FLESH:** The second type of false apostle is the minister of flesh. His error is deeper, his damage to the body of Christ more widespread, and his accountability to God far greater.

This false one is adept at deception and often ends up fooling himself as well as myriads of others around him. Since he has no true, godly, apostolic call, his motivation for walking in the shoes of an apostle comes from another source: self. He is not as concerned with promoting or magnifying God as much as exalting himself. He is not as interested in building God's body or Church as he is anxious to raise his own name and ministry. He is not a pioneer but a leech.

False apostle #2 exalts himself rather than God.

In essence, he is a self-raised, self-proclaimed minister of flesh. Rather than being an ambassador for God, he represents himself and indulges in works of flesh (such as false signs, wonders, or miracles) to promote his ministry and credibility. He is not in submission to the Lord or to the true Church. Since he is not in submission to God, he does not have the authority of God. He just goes out on his own behalf, in his own name, bringing trouble and deception with him.

3. THE REPROBATE: At the third level of error in apostleship there is the truly corrupt minister, the agent of Satan. If a false apostle has slid too far along the path of the reprobate, he is neither the premature minister of God nor the errant agent of self. Instead, his calling is from the ungodly one, Satan. *(Acts 5:37; 1 Timothy 4:1).* If truly given over to evil, he is the lackey of the unholy. He represents the kingdom of darkness, is given its authority, and acts on its behalf. As a slave of sin, he promotes heresy and brings confusion. This false apostle's ultimate purpose is not to promote God's kingdom or even his own, but to usher in the antichrist.

In espousing error and heresy, this false apostle goes beyond where others have gone, but he does so scripturally, not geographically. He builds **False apostle #3 promotes the kingdom of darkness.** unholy empires on private revelation, personal dreams, or visions of his own mind. He strays far beyond the boundary of the Word. He often subtly changes the Word or preaches his revelation of a new word, never realizing or caring that there is no such thing as a new Word.

45

Thus, instead of being a steward of the Scriptures of God, he becomes a creator of his own directives for men. He pulls down and destroys the work of other worthy, godly ministers of the Word, then lays a false foundation on which he builds the counterfeit church of antichrist.

The Word succinctly describes these masquerade ministers.

1 Timothy 4:1-2 (TAB) states:

But the (Holy) Spirit distinctly and expressly declares that in latter times some will turn away from the faith, giving attention to deluding and seducing spirits and doctrines that demons teach through the hypocrisy and pretensions of liars whose consciences are seared (cauterized)....

False apostles give attention to the doctrines of demons. In the end times, they will turn from the faith and be used in hypocrisy and deception to disseminate evil.

If we now recognize that there are three levels of false apostleship, the immature, of self, and of Satan, then all three must be recognized as just that—false. The Word rings true of these false apostles:

For such men are false apostles—spurious, counterfeits—deceitful workmen, masquerading as apostles (special messengers) of Christ, the Messiah. And it is no wonder, for Satan himself masquerades as an angel of light, so it is not surprising if his servants also masquerade as ministers of righteousness.

[But] their end will correspond with their deeds. 2
Corinthians 11:13-15 (TAB)

WARNING

While the problem of false apostleship abounds today, it
is by no means a new one. Even in the first century, the
apostle Paul was all too well aware that false apostles
were already infiltrating the Church. His warning still rings
out:

But [now] I am fearful lest that even as the serpent
beguiled Eve by his cunning, so your minds may be
corrupted and seduced from wholehearted and
sincere and pure devotion to Christ. For [you seem
readily to endure it] if a man comes and preaches
another Jesus that the One we preached, or if you
receive a different spirit from the [Spirit] you [once]
received, or a different gospel from the one you
[then] received and welcomed. You tolerate [all
that] well enough! 2 Corinthians 11:3-4 (TAB)

And just who were those that were presenting to the
unwary another Jesus, a different Spirit, and a different
gospel? In the very next verse, the perpetrators of evil are
very clearly identified: *"Yet I consider myself as in no way*
inferior to these (precious) extra-super [false] apostles"
(2 Corinthians 11:5 TAB).

Was Paul speaking of just the newly birthed Church?
Was his concern about the presentation of falsehood peculiar only to the first century body of Christ? Could this
be a problem in today's Church too?

47

The Word not only assures us that it could be but it also warns us that this would be an on going evil. Again it is Paul who could so clearly see the danger:

> I know that after I am gone ferocious wolves will get in among you, not sparing the flock; even from among your own selves men will come to the front, who by saying perverse (distorted and corrupt) things will endeavor to draw away the disciples after them [to their own party]. Acts 20:29-30 (TAB)

From these verses we can learn that false apostles and those they affect most are in the Church. Outsiders are not responsible for sending false apostles into the Church. The world is not responsible for the susceptibility to false ministry of some weak sheep. Outsiders would immediately be spotted as ignorant of God's ways and unlearned in His Word; they would be dismissed as leaders of the sheep. Sadly, false apostles and those willing to listen to them have arisen among misguided Christians whose ears and hearts are tuned to rebellion.

All of this, the preaching of a wrong word, the falling away from God, the separating from the true Church and the building up of a different, false church leads directly to one known consequence. This was spoken of as a sign of the final days.

> Let no one deceive you by any means; for that Day will not come unless the falling away comes first, and the man of sin is revealed, the son of perdition. 2 Thessalonians 2:3 (NKJV)

Now the Spirit expressly says that in latter times some will depart from the faith, giving heed to deceiving spirits and doctrines of demons. 1 Timothy 4:1 (NKJV)

THE FRUIT OF FALSE APOSTLES

APOSTASY: The direct result of false apostleship is apostasy. According to *Funk and Wagnalls Dictionary*, apostasy is an English word derived from two Greek words. As previously mentioned, the preposition *apo* means "from" or "away" and *stasis* means "to stand." Apostasy, then, means "to stand aside" or "stand away from." It is a desertion. Concerning the Church, it is a desertion of the true God and an abandonment of true faith and godly principles accompanied with a desire on the part of some to pull others into the same error.

False apostles take a stand away from the main flock. They will not live with the flock or under submission to the shepherds of the flock. Instead, they stand near the door of the fold of the flock and call out to unwary sheep, luring and enticing them to come and join them. Also they isolate unsuspecting sheep in the field and bleat empty promises and false doctrine to them, leading the gullible lambs away from the true flock and into that of the false apostle. Then they lock the door behind the unsuspecting, deluded lambs and become their warden or controller rather than their guardian or caretaker.

The false apostle's goal is apostasy.

Whether as an active agent of destruction or as an innocent dupe, the result is the same—apostasy. What began as one standing apart and wooing the unsuspecting has led to a group of people standing apart. This is rejection of the true Way. It is rejection of Christ. It is apostasy.

Today we live in those last days spoken of in Scripture. False apostles are even now separating the flock by preaching a false word full of empty, futile promises. They are speaking to and leading away those no longer willing to hear the truth.

> For the time is coming when [people] will not tolerate (endure) sound and wholesome instruction, but having ears itching [for something pleasing and gratifying], they will gather to themselves one teacher after another to a considerable number, chosen to satisfy their own liking and to foster the errors they hold, and will turn aside from hearing the truth and wander off into myths and man-made fictions. 2 Timothy 2:4:3-4 (TAB)

The misguided do not always recognize the voice of their Master. They are all too willing to hear and respond to another voice. They don't truly know the Word and haven't truly left the world. They asked Jesus to be their Savior but don't recognize Him as Lord. Without too much effort, the false apostle can cut them off from the flock and lead them all too willingly to new pastures.

It is the professing Christians from whom and to whom deception will come. By its very definition, apostasy cannot come from or affect those in the world because they do not know God's truth, and apostasy is a falling away from, a desertion of, or a stance apart from that truth. Since apostasy is so destructive to the Church, Christ's body is warned to be on guard for wolves who will not spare the flock.

This situation is similar to one that existed many years ago. In heaven there was a great falling away from worship of the true God. In pride and rebellion, Lucifer wanted the angels to worship him *(Isaiah 14:13-14)*. Due to his efforts to seek his own power and glory, Almighty God cast Lucifer out of heaven *(Ezekiel 28:16)*. Now known as Satan, he is still trying to be the object of worship—this time mankind's. Using lies, deception, and the manipulations of his false apostles, Satan is trying to lead the elect into rebellion and apostasy so that they will fulfill his plan and worship him.

OUR RESPONSE TO THE FALSE APOSTLE

Since the Bible so clearly describes apostasy and those involved in it, each saint must choose carefully whom he will listen to and follow. There are many voices raised to deceive, so each of us must learn to guard ourselves from error.

KNOW THE WORD: First, for protection, each must know the Word *(Ephesians 4:13-16)*. A passing acquaintance with God's Word is not enough. Each must thoroughly treat himself to its riches, pour through its eternity, and, by so doing, strike up a lasting relationship with

Jesus, who is the Word made flesh. His Word is truth. No saint can stand before God and claim ignorance when His Word is available to all. Each is personally accountable to Him for it. Ignorance or blaming error on others is no excuse for walking in apostasy.

BE CONSECRATED TO GOD: Next, the saints cannot stay among known, deliberate error (*1 Timothy 6:5*). A little leaven leavens the whole lump. We cannot continue to remain exposed to false words and expect to remain untouched. If we walk in error, sooner or later, we will fall into it. As apostasy spreads, we will get caught up in it. Now, more than ever, we must seek holiness and consecration unto God to remain pure.

WEAR GOD'S ARMOR: In order to protect ourselves from spiritual wolves, we must be sure our God-given armor is in place. One piece, the helmet, specifically guards our head (*Ephesians 6:17*). Our helmet of salvation keeps us clear-headed and helps us avert confusion. If properly worn, it saves us from casting off salvation in order to once again follow the bringer of bondage.

CORRECT KNOWN ERROR: We must have the boldness to expose falsehood and heresy (*Galatians 1:6-9*). The enemy is out to destroy. In these last hours he's attacking more than ever before. He, the author of lies and deception, must be revealed in his evil work. In so doing, it is not required of us to pull down men, but it is required that we rid ourselves of the ungodly words of men and the evil works of Satan. We cannot be slack in doing so.

We must petition God for a generous and merciful outpouring of discernment. He is the giver of all good gifts (*James 1:17*), and we need the ability to distinguish between good, human, and evil spirits as never before. It is imperative to know by what spirit a man or ministry is operating. Since our natural mind is unable to reveal this to us, we need the wisdom and guidance of the Holy Spirit who is the Spirit of truth; it is He who reveals the power behind the spirits of men.

TEST: Finally, we must not believe every spirit; rather, we must test the spirits to see if they proceed from God (*1 John 4:1-6*). Particularly, we must test the spirits of those who are so greatly influencing the body of Christ today. Those who are true apostles will rejoice that our obedience to the Word of God will prove their ministry sound.

Long ago, the Church in Ephesus received great commendation from the Lord because they had done just that. They tested the spirits of those who claimed they were apostles and found them to be liars (*Ephesians 2: 1,2,7*).

Is today's church any different?

Don't we have the same need to test those who claim to be apostles?

If we want to receive the Lord's commendation, hadn't we, His Church, also better discern the truth about our apostles?

THE APOSTLES

	THE TRUE	THE FALSE
CHARACTER:	• sent out • holy/honorable • honest • people of right conduct • people of integrity • walk under and in Godly authority • endure	• go out • hold only a form of piety • masters of deception and lies • seducers • have no integrity rebel against God • flee/guilt
PURPOSE:	• lay the true foundation and build the Church • represent God	• lay a false foundation and build a false Church • represent self or Satan
LEVELS:	• **THE GRACE:** those who enjoy the unusual or who initiate new projects • **THE MINISTRY:** those who are sent out on missions trips and find they adapt to new cultures easily • **THE APOSTLE:** those sent forth from the local Church to the world to introduce Jesus and the kingdom of God and to establish His Church in areas that do not know or acknowledge Him	• those who teach error or try to build his own kingdom instead of God's within the Church • those who feel thwarted in their local Church and who go out without being sent out to start their own "church" or ministry • those who lay a false foundation for a false church that honors a false god
METHODS:	• delcare holy doctrine • integrate people with God • prepare the dwell in place of God • prepare for the return of Christ	• spread a false word • lead people away from God • build their own empires • usher in the antichrist

PROPHETS: THE TRUE

"And He Himself gave some to be...prophets...."
Ephesians 4:11 (NKJV)

The second ascension gift that Jesus gave to the Church was that of prophet. To equip the saints to minister, to edify His body until both a spiritual oneness and the knowledge of Christ are attained and until maturity is evidenced, Jesus sent His Church prophets.

Like the word for apostle, the word prophet can be understood through the Greek language. It comes from the Greek word *prophemi*. The prefix of this word, *pro*, means "forth;" the word *phemi* means "to tell," "to speak," or "to shine." Thus a prophet is one who speaks forth. He tells it like it is.

A prophet is not simply a pastor or preacher who regularly expounds the Word of God to an assembly. He is a special speaker with a special word for a special person, people, time, age, place, or circumstance.

TWO PHASES OF PROPHESYING

A prophet is a spokesman for God. He is God's mouthpiece. He points out the way to go. A prophet is one to whom some of the mysteries and secrets of God have been revealed (*Amos 3:7*) and who then is commissioned to communicate those revelations to others (Amos 3:8). A prophet knows the very heartbeat of God and, at an appropriate time, sets the trumpet to his mouth to announce it publicly.

A prophet therefore has a two-fold ministry. He is both a receiver and a giver.

RECEIVER: As a receiver, a prophet has direct access to the counsels of heaven (*1 Kings 17:1; Jeremiah 23:18*). He

A prophet receives revelation. is one to whom God reveals His will by direct revelation or through dreams or visions (*Numbers 12:6*). Once called a seer, a prophet sees into the spiritual realm; he sees things others don't see and thereby gains insight into the ways and will of God (*Habakkuk 1:1*). Also, he hears things others do not hear in the divine courts and counsels of God (*Isaiah 48:6*).

GIVER: As a giver, a prophet is charged to share or communicate these insights with others (*Jeremiah 1:5-7; 1 Peter 4: 10-11*). After walking in the councils of heaven or hearing heavenly things, he comes back to earth to utter a "thus sayeth the Lord."

For a true prophet, knowing the will of God is not

A prophet gives or reveals revelation. enough. A prophet feels a desperate need or has a burning desire to speak out and spread the message that was given to him in the counsels of God. With authority and clarity, he communicates the will of God to people. Having been taught by God, he speaks forth for God. He verbally announces God's message or publicly declares it through the written Word. Sometimes he even makes it known through music.

That prophecy incorporates receiving and giving can be seen in Moses' call to the prophetic office. God spoke to Moses and said:

> "Now therefore, behold, the cry of the children of Israel has come to Me, and I have also seen the oppression with which the Egyptians oppress them. Come now, therefore, **and I will send you to Pharaoh that you may bring My people, the children of Israel, out of Egypt.**" But Moses said to God, "Who am I that I should go to Pharaoh, and that I should bring the children of Israel out of Egypt?" So He said, "I will certainly be with you. And this shall be a sign to you that I have sent you: When you have brought the people out of Egypt, you shall serve God on this mountain." [emphasis added] Exodus 3:9-12 (NKJV)

God told Moses that He was going to deliver His children from bondage and that it was His intention to use Moses as His instrument of freedom. In thus revealing His will to Moses, Moses became the receiver of divine revelation and holy insight.

Then Moses was told to go and speak this revelation forth. In so doing, he would become a giver.

Go *and gather the elders of Israel together, and* **say to them,** *"The LORD God of your fathers, the God of Abraham, of Isaac, and of Jacob, appeared to me, saying, 'I have surely visited you and seen what is done to you in Egypt; and I have said I will bring you up out of the affliction of Egypt to the land of the Canaanites and the Hittites and the Amorites and the Perizzites and the Hivites and the Jebusites, to a land flowing with milk and honey.'" Then they will heed your voice; and you shall come, you and the elders of Israel, to the king of Egypt; and* **you shall say to him,** *"The LORD God of the Hebrews has met with us; and now, please, let us go three days' journey into the wilderness that we may sacrifice to the LORD our God."* [emphasis added] *Exodus 3:16-18 (NKJV)*

However, Moses did not want to do it. He did not believe he was equal to the job. He argued with God.

Then Moses said to the LORD, "O my Lord, I am not eloquent, neither before nor since You have spoken to Your servant; but I am slow of speech and slow of tongue." So the LORD said to him, "Who has made man's mouth? Or who makes the mute, the deaf, the seeing, or the blind? Have not I, the LORD? Now therefore, go, and I will be with your mouth and teach you what you shall say." Exodus 4:10-12 (NKJV)

Moses had received God's message but he did not want to be the messenger. He was, in his own eyes, only capable of functioning in half the office of prophet, that of receiving the revelation.

But God knew that was not enough. He knew His message, the expression of His will, must be spoken. He would not be denied in this.

> So the anger of the LORD was kindled against Moses, and He said: "Is not Aaron the Levite your brother? I know that he can speak well. And look, he is also coming out to meet you. When he sees you, he will be glad in his heart. Now you shall speak to him and put the words in his mouth. And I will be with your mouth and with his mouth, and I will teach you what you shall do. So he shall be your spokesman to the people. And he himself shall be as a mouth for you, and you shall be to him as God." Exodus 4:14-16 (NKJV)

God settled the issue by using Moses' brother Aaron as His voice. God would speak to Moses, Moses would speak to Aaron, and Aaron would speak to the Israelites. In that way, the full requirement of the office of prophet, the receiving of the revelation of God's will as well as the public expression of God's will, would be realized.

GOOD CHARACTER

A TRUE PROPHET IS A PERSON OF HONOR, INTEGRITY, AND SUBMISSION: Like an apostle, a prophet must be a person of highest character. Since he is otherworldly and spends a good deal of time in the courts of heaven, it must be with the greatest honesty and integrity that he communicates his divine knowledge. Since his job is to reveal God's will and to urge direct obedience to His ways, a prophet must walk in deepest submission to God. His life and visible testimony must be one of keeping strict, godly standards and walking in God's service to the best of his ability. Anything else would be blatant hypocrisy.

A TRUE PROPHET DENIES SELF AND PROMOTES GOD: A prophet is self-effacing. As a man of God, he is neither self-proclaiming nor self-aggrandizing. He understands that he speaks for God, not for self. He knows he must lead people to God not to self. The essence of this self-denial is realized in John the Baptist's statement concerning his relationship with Jesus: *"He must increase but I must decrease" (John 3:30 NKJV).*

A TRUE PROPHET DOES NOT COMPROMISE TRUTH: A true prophet does not know compromise. He sees things in black and white, not in gray. To him, a thing is either right or wrong. Either God said something or He didn't. Anything less than full compliance to the will and desires of God is not known or acceptable to a prophet.

A TRUE PROPHET PERSEVERES: A prophet's character must also include endurance. Many times he is walking in blind faith. Since he is so often rejected by men, for long periods of time God is the only one with whom he can truly commune and fellowship. Therefore a prophet must, at a very deep level, know His right standing with God. He must also place this relationship with God far above that of any relationship with people. In the long run, he knows that people will fail him but God will not.

A TRUE PROPHET IS NOT FOR SALE: Unlike Balaam (*Numbers* 22-24), a true prophet cannot be bought. Because his mouth is like a sharp sword and his determined words are piercing arrows of truth that penetrate the hearts of men, he is often hated.

A TRUE PROPHET WEEPS: Although others sometimes see him as intense, over committed to holiness, abrasive, and too bold, in the private corners of his heart, a prophet will be found weeping. Internally, his heart cries out before God day and night. The disparity between the revelation of the will of God in the courts of heaven and the reality of its outworking on earth among the sinful and indifferent breaks a prophet's heart. Like Jeremiah over Israel (*Jeremiah* 14:17) and Jesus over Jerusalem (*Luke* 19:41), he continuously sobs out his agony.

WHAT DOES A PROPHET DO?

Prophets, for good reasons and bad, are the most mentioned and controversial of the spiritual gifts and ministries today. Everyone, saved or unsaved, seems to have his or her own idea of who prophets are and what they should be doing. Relying on man's opinions about prophecy rather than learning God's Word concerning prophecy has led to problems. Ignorance and manipulation also have done much to harm the prophetic ministry. As a result, prophets have often been discredited in the end times Church.

A prophet inspires and stimulates.

To return prophecy to the position it should occupy, saints must be willing to let the Word teach them. One thing that can be learned from diligent search of the Scriptures in that the goals of a prophet are threefold:

A TRUE PROPHET MOTIVATES: Through exhortation, he stirs things up and gets saints moving in godly ways. He inspires people and urges them to take action.

A TRUE PROPHPET RESTORES: One with the office of prophet calls into line that which is out of order. He does so by identifying evil or spotlighting error and wrongdoing and insisting on its correction or removal. He is not concerned with what is popular, but only with what is right according to God and His Word. In proclaiming error, he restores His truth; in declaring God's will, he restores His way.

A TRUE PROPHET LEADS PEOPLE TO GOD: All that a true prophet says comes from God *(John 3:34)* and is for the glory of God. He is heard crying, "Repent, repent!" to deafened ears all around him and is seen trying to lead them back to God.

A true prophet leads people to God.

He is the seer leading the blind into the ways of God.

CONTRASTING APOSTLES AND PROPHETS

While there are similarities in apostles and prophets as founders and builders of God's Church, there are also major differences in the two offices. As has been learned, God's apostle is one who has been sent out to lay the foundation of the Church. Ultimately, as part of the five-fold ministry, it is the goal of God's prophet to build on that foundation; he is to motivate, restore, mend, and guide the Church that has been founded on the Rock.

> Now, therefore, you are no longer strangers and foreigners, but fellow citizens with the saints and members of the household of God, having been built on the foundation of the apostles and prophets, Jesus Christ Himself being the chief cornerstone. Ephesians 2:19-20 (NKJV)

A true apostle starts from scratch and lays the sure foundation of Jesus Christ. However, at times, a true prophet may sometimes find that a false apostle has been at work, one who has laid a false foundation. Or, he may find that the structure that has been built on a good foundation is bad. Therefore, before any further building can take place, he must make people aware of error and call out for reform. A prophet is commissioned, if need be, to root out and pull down, to destroy and throw down first. Then when wrong is made right, he can go on to build and to plant (Jeremiah 1:10). In other words, the apostle lays a foundation; if his work wasn't founded right or that which was build on a right foundation is wrong, the prophet can be instrumental in tearing down the works of flesh or evil, making corrections, and raising a true house of God.

Along with the apostle, the prophet builds the true Church.

GOD'S MAIL CARRIER

While an apostle has been compared to an ambassador, it is quite appropriate to liken a prophet with a mail carrier. In the world, a mail carrier is given a communication from one called a sender and asked to deliver it to one intended as recipient. The mail carrier does not originate or make up the message. Nor is the mail carrier responsible for the attitude or behavior of the one receiving or rejecting the communication. He is simply the agent by which it came.

In the kingdom of God, a prophet is one who delivers a message too. It is a divine message from God to man. The true prophet does not originate the message; God does. He is in no way responsible for its contents; God is. Since the prophet is speaking on behalf of Another, he should not receive glory or praise for the message. Nor should he receive blame. As a messenger, he is not responsible for the attitudes, responses, or reactions of those receiving the message. Acceptance or rejection, obedience or disobedience lies squarely on the shoulders of the recipients (*Deuteronomy 13:1-5; 18:19*).

A true prophet delivers God's message.

LEVELS OF THE PROPHETIC

1. THE GRACE: First, in the local Church, there is the grace (charisma) of prophecy. This is a unique message applicable to a particular situation at a particular time. This gentle nudging of the Holy Spirit could be a revelation received and then expressed by a saint who never prophesied before and who may never be asked to do so again. Or, it can be a very occasional word that, if handled in a trustworthy manner by the one prophesying, may or may not lead to the ministry of prophecy.

2. THE MINISTRY GIFT: Second, in the local Church there is the ministry gift (*charisma*) of prophecy given to the Church by the Holy Spirit (*1 Corinthians 12:10*). In this ministry, the Holy Spirit reveals a word that He then wants expressed to the body through the saint to whom He gave it.

How blessed is the Church that the Lord would urge all saints, with care and adherence to His word and ways, to desire to prophesy (1 Corinthians 14:1).

3. THE PROPHET: Finally, there is the third area or-level of prophecy: the ascension gift (*doma*) or the office of prophet. This was given to the Church by Jesus Christ rather than by the Spirit and is for some, not for all (*Ephesians 4:11*).

One way of expressing the difference between one with the office of prophet and those with the ministry grace or gift of prophecy is that all prophets prophesy, but not all who prophesy are prophets. In addition, the one with the office of prophet ministers not only to the local body but also to the universal Church.

The office of prophet encompasses a great deal more than the grace or ministry gift of prophecy. In addition to edifying, exhorting, and comforting, a prophet of God is charged to rebuke, warn, and correct in order to reveal error. This is the forth-telling aspect of prophecy. Its goal is to reform or change. Also, a prophet has authority to guide, direct, or preach in order to reveal truth. This is the foretelling aspect of prophecy. Its goal is to lead saints to God.

HOW IS A PROPHET CHOSEN?

SOVEREIGN CHOICE: The chief priests, scribes, and elders once asked Jesus by whose authority He did things (*Luke 20:2*). It would be well to ask the same question about today's prophets. By whose authority does a true prophet speak forth? From where does he get the authority to do what he does?

Like an apostle, a true prophet is not his own. His ability is from, his dependence is on, and his direction is toward the Godhead. He becomes a prophet by God's choice alone (*Jeremiah 1:5-7*).

First, he is admitted into the divine, heavenly counsels by the grace of God. Then, in order for God's revelations to be given to the Church, he is given the ascension gift of prophet by Jesus (*Ephesians 4:11*). Finally, his ministry is accomplished or empowered by the Holy Spirit (*2 Peter 1:20-21*). When this anointing on a prophet is recognized by others, he is raised up and placed into this office in the Church.

When Jesus left the earth, He sent the Holy Spirit (*John 16:7*) to the saints still on earth. His express purpose for doing so was:

> But when He, the Spirit of Truth (the truth-giving Spirit) comes, He will guide you into all the truth—

the whole, full truth. For He will not speak His own message—on His own authority—but He will tell whatever He hears [from the Father, He will give the message that has been given to Him] and He will announce and declare to you the things that are to come—that will happen in the future. John 16:13 (TAB)

Thus it is seen that a prophet's authority comes from the Godhead. God allows him to hear and see, Jesus calls him into the ministry that allows him to express God's words, and the Holy Spirit empowers him to speak truth.

THE AUTHORITY OF THE WORD: Additionally, a prophet is in submission to the authority of the Word of God. In speaking forth, a prophet may, by the power of the Spirit, perform miracles. Sometimes signs and wonders accompany the proclamation of the Word. In a way, these validate the messenger; they show that God's grace rests on him. However, the message is of more importance than the messenger. A prophet's word must always line up with God's Word. It is Scripture, not miracles, that truly validates the message.

It must be understood that the Bible is a book of prophecy. It speaks forth Jesus. From Genesis to Revelation, the prophetic Word reveals Jesus. Since all prophecy is subject to judgment by other prophets, so too, any word spoken as prophecy is subject to the prophetic Word. God's Word is always the final judge of truth.

MOSES, AN OLD TESTAMENT PROPHET

In Old Testament times, a prophet was one who foresaw and spoke of the salvation of man through the redemptive work of Jesus. As he did so, he predicted Jesus' birth, life, and death. In one way or another, his words led to and revealed Christ. It was Jesus Himself who declared that the Old Testament prophesied and taught of him: "Then beginning with Moses and (throughout) all the prophets, He went on explaining and interpreting to them in all the Scriptures the things concerning and referring to Himself" (*Luke 24:27 TAB*).

While the Old Testament prophets foresaw salvation coming through the mercy of Christ and looked forward to its fulfillment at the cross, the New Testament prophets proclaimed the salvation that had been accomplished by Him. They were on the other side of the cross but their words and their revelations still pointed to Jesus.

While the Old Testament lists several men who preceded him as prophets, it seems that the beginning of the prophetic office as we know it today began with Moses. Continuing his story, when God rescued the Hebrew children and delivered them out of Egypt, they soon found themselves camped at the foot of Mount Sinai. There God desired to do a new thing. Rather than seeming to be stern or aloof, He desired to meet with and talk with His people in direct fellowship.

He appeared to them on the mountain with smoke and fire, thunder and lightning, and the sound of a trumpet (*Exodus 19:16*). The Lord then issued the Ten Commandments to the people with whom He wanted to dwell. However, *"....all the people witnessed the thunderings, the lightning flashes, the sound of the trumpet, and the mountain smoking; and when the people saw it, they trembled and stood afar off"* (Exodus 20:18 NKJV).

Their reaction to God was not delight or rejoicing in His presence. Rather, it was outright fear. As a result, they said to Moses, *"You speak with us and we will hear; but let not God speak with us, lest we die"* (Exodus 20:19 NKJV).

From then on, Moses became the man in the middle. Unlike his brother Aaron who, as an Old Testament priest, stood between man and God, Moses, as an Old Testament prophet, stood between God and man.

JESUS, A NEW TESTAMENT PROPHET

While the Old Testament described the emergence of a man as a prophet of God, it also prophesied of a coming One who would be the prophet of God.

> *The Lord your God will raise up for you a prophet from the midst of your brethren, like me [Moses]; to him you shall listen...I will raise up for them a prophet from among their brethren, like you, and will put My words in his mouth; and he shall speak to them all that I command him. Deuteronomy 18:15,18 (TAB)*

The New Testament expressly identifies Jesus as this Prophet:

> *Thus Moses said to the forefathers, The Lord God will raise up for you a Prophet from among your*

brethren as [He raised up] me; Him you shall listen
to and understand by hearing, and heed in all things
whatever He tells you. And it shall be that every soul
that does not listen to and understand by hearing
and heed that Prophet shall be utterly exterminat-
ed from among the people. Acts 3:22-23 (TAB)

With all authority and knowing His Father's will as
none before had known it, Jesus came to earth from
heavenly places, lived here as a man, and expressed and
did that divine will.

Jesus said to them, "My food is to do the will of Him
who sent Me, and to finish His work." John 4:34
(NKJV)

I can of Myself do nothing. As I hear, I judge; and
My judgment is righteous, because I do not seek
My own will but the will of the Father who sent Me.
John 5:30 (NKJV)

This is the will of the Father who sent Me, that of all
He has given Me I should lose nothing, but should
raise it up at the last day. And this is the will of Him
who sent Me, that everyone who sees the Son and
believes in Him may have everlasting life; and I will
raise him up at the last day. John 6:39-40 (NKJV)

In so doing, He directly, perfectly fulfilled the role of
prophet. In His prophetic office, He walked in the fullest
aspect of His calling.

As a prophet, Jesus exhorted or stirred up: *"You are the salt of the earth...You are the light of the world"* *(Matthew 5:13-14 NKJV).*

As a prophet, Jesus exhorted or stirred up: "Let your light so shine before men, that they may see your good works and glorify your Father in heaven" (Matthew 5:16 NKJV).

As a prophet, Jesus comforted:

Blessed are the poor in spirit, for theirs is the kingdom of heaven. Blessed are those who mourn, for they shall be comforted. Blessed are the meek for they shall inherit the earth. Blessed are those who hunger and thirst for righteousness, for they shall be filled. Blessed are the merciful, for they shall obtain mercy. Blessed are the pure in heart, for they shall see God. Blessed are the peacemakers, for they shall be called sons of God. Blessed are those who are persecuted for righteousness's sake, for theirs is the kingdom of heaven. (Matthew 5:3-10 NKJV)

As a prophet, Jesus warned: *"Remember therefore from where you have fallen; repent and do the first works, or I will come to you quickly and remove your lampstand from its place—unless you repent"* *(Revelations 2:5 NKJV).*

As a prophet, Jesus rebuked: *"Hypocrites! Well did Isaiah prophesy about you, saying: 'These people draw near to Me with their mouth, and honor Me with their lips, but their heart is far from Me. And in vain they worship Me, teaching as doctrines the commandments of men'"* *(Matthew 15:7-9 NKJV).*

As a prophet, Jesus judged:

And Jesus said, "For judgment I have come into this world, that those who do not see may see, and that those who see may be made blind." (John 9:39 NKJV)

You are of you father the devil, and the desires of your father you want to do. He was a murderer from the beginning, and does not stand in the truth, because there is no truth in him. When he speaks a lie, he speaks from his own resources, for he is a liar and the father of it. John 8:44 (NKJV)

As a prophet, Jesus corrected: "You have heard that it was said, 'An eye for an eye and a tooth for a tooth.' **But I tell you** not to resist an evil person. But whoever slaps you on your right cheek, turn the other to him also" [emphasis added] (Matthew 5:38-39 NKJV).

As a prophet, Jesus revealed:

....the kingdom of heaven is at hand. Matthew 4:17 (NKJV)

The Spirit of the Lord is upon Me, because He has anointed Me to preach the gospel to the poor. He has sent Me to heal the brokenhearted, to preach the deliverance to the captives and recovery of sight to the blind, to set at liberty those who are oppressed, to preach the acceptable year of the Lord. Luke 4:18-19 (NKJV)

As a prophet, Jesus guided: "Behold, I send the Promise of My Father upon you; but tarry in the city of Jerusalem until are endued with power from on high" *(Luke 24:49 NKJV)*.

As a prophet, Jesus predicted: *"Destroy this temple, and in three days I will raise it up" (John 2:19 NKJV)*.

As a prophet, Jesus called for repentance: *"Repent...."* *(Matthew 4:17 NKJV)*.

As a prophet, Jesus also inspired, motivated, restored, and led people to Himself *(Luke 9:18)*. Gracefully yet powerfully, honorably yet honestly, He fulfilled His office. In so doing, He became the perfect pattern or role model for all those who would follow in His footsteps.

FIRST CENTURY PROPHETS

In the New Testament, several men and women are specifically designated as prophets or prophetesses. Among these are Anna *(Luke 2:36)*, Peter *(2 Peter 1:1-2)*, and Paul *(1 Timothy 4:1)*. They too learned and spoke forth the word and will of God. Perhaps the early Church's most well known prophetic voice belongs to a man who, in body but not in spirit, was held captive on an isle called Patmos. His name is John.

In the writings of John, author of the book of Revelation, there is undeniably a clear flow of prophecy. It is an entire book of prophetic revelation and is a link between the first century, the twenty-first century, and the future. All elements of prophecy are incorporated into it. It declares that it is the revelation of Jesus Christ *(Revelations 1:1)*, includes a prediction of the coming King, the new heaven, earth, and holy city *(Revelations 21:1)* and issues a warning, *"Behold, I am coming quickly!" (Revelations 22:7 NKJV)*.

As God warned us then through His prophet, He is warning us now through His prophets.

TWENTY-FIRST CENTURY PROPHETS

Since God had not revealed all that was to be revealed when Jesus, the Prophet, left earth, He knew men would continue to need to know the word, ways, and will of God. *Romans 2:18a (TAB)* tells us, *"And know and understand His will and discerningly approve the better things and have a sense of what is vital."* Although in context this Scripture is a part of a rebuke, it nevertheless defines the needs of disciples today. This need is met, in part at least, through holy prophets.

God's will has never changed. He wanted man to be saved, sanctified, taught, disciplined, and grow to maturity in the first century, and He wants it for everyone today. The work of a prophet is to express this will and to motivate people to do that will.

Before Jesus left, He established His Church to be the earthly agent for carrying out His Father's will. From the Church, He gave to the Church the prophet to reveal and declare that will. As with the apostles, although the first century prophets who walked in the office have died, yet the gift goes on. Knowing the will of God comes in part through proper administration of the prophetic gift.

While the prophet may be the vessel of God by which the prophetic word is spoken forth, the agent of the inspiration of any true prophetic word is still the Holy Spirit. *"Now He who searches the hearts knows what the mind of the Spirit is, because He makes intercession for the saints according to the will of God" (Romans 8:27 NKJV)*. God reveals, the Holy Spirit breathes life on the revelation, and the prophet speaks forth.

Just as Jesus was foreseen in the Old Testament as the Prophet and identified as such in the New Testament, so too prophesying was foretold in the old and confirmed in the new.

> *And it shall come to pass afterward that I will pour out My Spirit on all flesh; **your sons and your daughters shall prophesy,** your old men shall dream dreams, your young men shall see visions. [emphasis added] Joel 2:28 (NKJV)*

> *And on My menservants and on **My** maidservants I will pour out My Spirit in those days; **and they shall prophesy.** [emphasis added] Acts 2:18 (NKJV)*

Today God is moving over all the earth. He is even now sending out His true prophets to proclaim His will and lead saints into a deeper commitment to Him. Once more, the trumpets are sounding. As in other days, He is revealing His secrets to His prophets and telling them to prophesy. The Church needs to be warned, alert, and ready to respond to the sound of His trumpet.

Like an apostle, a prophet is to build upon the foundation of God's Church (*Ephesians 2:20*). Sadly, there are many in the Church who deny the validity and the authority of the prophetic office. Since so many have been burned by so much abuse, in many areas this ministry is entirely rejected. Those short-sighted ones who are denying God's vessels the expression of their ministry must grasp the truth of God's Word: *"Where there is no revelation, the people cast off restraint"* (Proverbs 29:18 NKJV).

If our seers cannot tell us what they see, the Church will not become a well-equipped Church. If prophets are ignored, she will not become a mature body. If the Church does not allow revelation that is freshly inspired by the Holy Spirit to breathe on it, that Church will die. Any church ignoring, denying, or suppressing revelation will fall (or perhaps has already fallen) into ritual rather than relationship with God. Ritual in the Church leads to sickness. Sickness with no infilling of life leads to death. Death reigns, all for the lack of prophets.

PROPHECY IN THE LOCAL CHURCH

The Word sets forth several regulations that must be followed in manifesting either the grace or ministry gift of prophecy in the local Church:

PROPHECY MUST EDIFY, EXHORT, AND COMFORT: First, any word so given in a local Church is to be expressed in a special way: *"But he who prophesies speaks edification, and exhortation, and comfort to men"*(1 Corinthians 14:3 NKJV).

The prophets of old used to thunder their messages, and some in today's Church have tried to add credence to their words by emulating them. However, at the grace or ministry level of the gift of prophecy, God has clearly indicated that any who are speaking for Him must do so in a way that lifts and loves. Even if the word to be spoken seems negative, with a little practice it can be said in a positive way. There is no need to reveal too much publicly or to embarrass the one receiving the word.

The words of the one who prophesies must uplift and encourage.

PROPHECY MUST BE GIVEN IN A GODLY MANNER: God's Word states that when a saint is exercising the ministry gift of prophecy, the word spoken is subject to the one speaking it *(1 Corinthians 14:32)*. This means that the one prophesying does not have to blurt out his message at inappropriate times or in questionable, bizarre, interruptive, or offensive ways. If the one prophesying feels he is subject to a spirit forcing him to speak out such a word, that dominating spirit is not of God and no word should be spoken. If the one speaking a word does so in the flesh with message and manner designed to draw attention to the speaker, that one should be asked to keep silent. God will not contradict His own call to order *(1 Corinthians 14:40)* just to have a so-called prophetic word spoken.

PROPHECY MUST BE JUDGED: As a final admonition, t is an absolute rule of God that any spoken word of prophecy must be judged. First, a prophecy must be judged by

The words of one who prophesies must be judged.

the one receiving the word. The receiver must agree that the prophecy is something that God has begun stirring in his heart and the receiver must know in her heart that the word is credible enough to be prayed about, or, if necessary, put on the shelf for awhile.

Second, it must be judged by others (*1 Corinthians 14:29*). In the Greek the word for others is allas. It means another in number but of the same kind. In essence, prophecy must be judged by others trained to discern the true or the false in the prophetic.

Therefore, in a local Church gathering, if one with a grace or ministry gift of prophecy wants to give a word and there are no others with similar gifting to judge the word, some precautions are in order. Perhaps the one receiving the word could have another listen to the word as it is given to verify what was said. The word could then be taken to one who has prophetic gifting to be judged. Or perhaps a recording could be made of the word so it could be presented for judgment. Finally, if there are no others with a prophetic grace or ministry gift present at a gathering, perhaps no prophetic word should be spoken at that time.

TWO ASPECTS OF PROPHESYING

As mentioned, there are two aspects of prophecy to consider. The first is forth-telling. Here the prophet speaks forth truth. In a clear, decisive way he speaks that which is on God's heart. He speaks a current word to a person or to the Church. The second is fore-telling. Here the prophet utters prediction or guidance. After God reveals to him a peek into the future, a prophet makes known beforehand things that are about to happen.

PROBLEMS WITH FORTHTELLING

Concerning the forth-telling aspect of the office of prophet, the additional responsibilities of rebuking, warning,

A prophet corrects error in the Church. or correcting error have not been well understood or accepted by many in the body of Christ. These saints view rebuking or correcting in a negative way. What they fail to realize is that although something seems at first to be a negative word, if it leads to positive obedience, to the repentance of a sinful situation, or to the restoration of a saint, then in the long run, speaking an unpopular word will have had a positive effect on the Church and the saints therein.

Contrary to the Word of God, saints in some parts of the body of Christ are being taught that correction is not a valid function of the office of prophet. They are being taught that God is only a God of love and therefore any word of rebuke is out of order. Sadly, occasionally a prophet uttering a proper, God-inspired word of rebuke is himself rebuked for daring to speak the truth. Such is error! God's Word is inerrant and authoritative. It declares that God disciplines those He loves (Hebrews 23:6). Should His Church leaders do any less?

In a passage outlining the disservice to His people by her prophets, priests, and princes, God testifies:

> *Her priests have done violence to My law and have profaned My holy things. They have made no distinction between the sacred and the secular, neither have they taught people the difference between the unclean and the clean, and I have hid their eyes from My Sabbaths, and I am profaned among them. Ezekiel 22:26 (TAB)*

From days of old, in both the Church and the world, men have had trouble admitting that God is a just God as well as a loving, merciful one. They don't want to acknowledge their need for righteousness through the blood of Jesus, and so they only seek expressions of His love. Men do not want to be accountable to holy God for unholy actions, and they therefore concentrate only on the loving, gentle characteristics of God's nature. They seek an outward expression of forgiveness while forgetting that forgiveness is not the result of compromise or of denying the unpleasant reality of attitude or behavior. True forgiveness is the result of conviction of sin, of repentance, of confession of sin, and of reconciliation with the Father in heart or spirit.

God has clearly included words of admonition and correction in the responsibilities that He has placed on the shoulders of the prophets. All must remember that when a true prophet issues a timely word of warning or of judgment, it is not the prophet's opinion or judgment; it is God's.

PROBLEMS WITH FORETELLING

While problems are present in the corrective or forth-tell-ing aspect of prophecy, it is without question that prob-lems abound in the predictive or foretelling side of proph-ecy as well.

PROPHESYING IS NOT FORTUNE TELLING: There is a general misunderstanding among many that prophecy is equated with fortune telling. Prophecy in its foretelling aspect can be, at least in part, a direction or a revelation concerning the future by God. Fortune telling, on the oth-er hand, is the sinful inquiring about and the evil revela-tion of future events by the ungodly.

To compare the two, prophecy is speaking forth a rev-elation of the will of God, while fortune telling is speaking forth a revelation of the will of flesh, a false god, or Satan. Prophecy is spoken through a chosen vessel of God, but fortune telling is spoken by a witch, a diviner, or other un-holy servant of the occult. Prophecy is given and inspired by the Holy Spirit, while fortune telling is inspired by a familiar or unholy spirit. Prophecy is blessed by God, but fortune telling is an abomination to Him. It is absolutely, in any form and at all times, forbidden to children of God (*Deuteronomy 18:10-12*).

NOT ALL PROPHECY IS PREDICTIVE: A second reason for such a plethora of problems in the predictive aspect of prophecy is that this area is overemphasized. Many magnify beyond all bounds this one facet of prophecy. While prediction is a valid function of prophecy, it is by no means the only one. It is but one of many possible expressions of a prophetic word.

It is not right to expect a word of prediction in all that a prophet says. Saints cannot claim he is in error if his words don't include prediction. The Church cannot limit an entire ministry to just one part of the whole. All must acknowledge as separate and distinct each aspect of prophecy. For example, one with the office of prophet may rebuke, but is not required to rebuke predictively; he just rebukes. He does not have to exhort predictively; he just exhorts. A prophet just speaks forth God's word in whatever way the message was given to him. Whether it includes prediction or not, if it is judged as correct, it is still a valid word from God.

THE GRACE OR MINISTRY GIFT OF PROHECY IS NOT THE OFFICE OF THE PROPHET: A third widespread and damaging problem in the realm of predictive prophecy is that some with only the grace or the prophetic ministry gift of the Holy Spirit are unjustifiably adding to their authority and incorporating correction and prediction in their ministry. Those with the ministry of prophecy should concentrate on edifying, exhorting, and comforting. Everything else, whether rebuking, warning, correcting, guiding, or predicting should be spoken only by a true prophet.

This crossing of lines of authority is leading to disaster in the body of Christ. It is impossible to estimate the damage done when two undiscerning people get married because a "prophet" told them to do so. Similarly, how many gullible saints are now facing fiscal shipwreck because of faulty financial direction given them by a so-called prophet of God?

Prophecy must be judged before it is accepted or acted upon. Also, they should reveal why those who are not prophets should not exercise the office of prophet. Instead of correction and help, their erroneous messages are actually causing confusion and bringing harm to the Church. Let each saint, before he should utter a questionable "thus sayeth the Lord," hear the word of warning: *"But I say to you that for every idle word men may speak, they will give account of it in the day of judgment"* (Matthew 12:36 NKJV).

A COMPARISON

	THE GRACE	THE MINISTRY	THE PROPHET
GREEK:	*charisma*	*charisma*	*doma*
REFERENCE:	1 Cor. 13.7 1 Cor. 14:3	1 Cor. 13:7 1 Cor. 14:3	Eph. 4:11
SOURCE:	the Spirit	the Spirit	Jesus
FROM WHOM:	all may prophesy	all may prophesy	some, not all are prophets
WHERE:	local Church	local Church and nearby community	local and universal Church
WHEN:	after God reveals His word and will	after God reveals His word and will	after God reveals His word and will
PURPOSE:	build the local Church	build the local and community Church	build the local, community, and universal Church
METHODS:	• edity • exhort • comfort	• edity • exhort • comfort	• edity • exhort • comfort • rebuke • warn judge/correct • refeal • call to repentance • guide • identity gifts and set them in the body of Christ • foretell/predict • forth-tell

PROPHETS: THE FALSE

"Beware of false prophets...." Matthew 7:15 (NKJV)

Without question, when the Lord sends that which is good among His people to help them in their search for or in their walk with Christ, the unholy will arise spreading that which is evil in order to deceive and lead astray. In so doing, a counterfeit of the true and good is raised up. Certainly this has proved true with prophecy.

God has raised up and is sending out those He has called to the ascension gift of prophet. They are to speak for Him and to speak forth His message. The enemy has also raised up and is sending out those who he has commissioned to speak his message. These are false prophets. They do not come from God, and they do not speak for Him. That false prophets exist and are clearly labeled as false messengers is easily validated in Scripture: *"Beware of false prophets, who come to you in sheep's clothing, but inwardly they are ravenous wolves"* (Matthew 7:15 NKJV).

Prophecy is the spoken gift that is the most often abused. Through ignorance or inexperience on the part of the immature but growing Christian or through the work of outright charlatans, prophecy has gained a questionable reputation in the body of Christ. Since the Word has clearly warned us that, *"....false christs and false prophets will arise, and they will show great signs and wonders, so as to deceive and lead astray, if possible, even the elect (God's chosen ones)"* (Matthew 24:24 TAB), we should learn the characteristics of the false ministries and ministers so that they can be identified and rejected.

BAD CHARACTER

As they differ in ministry, true prophets and false prophets also differ in character. It is sad but true that all who serve God do not serve Him honorably. Even within the ranks of the priesthood, there are some who are sinful (1 Samuel 2:12). As the message of the false prophet will not hold up to the scrutiny of the Lord or of discerning saints, neither will the messenger, the false prophet himself. If the message is out of order and doesn't flow from a heart established in God and built on His principles, the nature of the false messenger will not be right either. He has a many-flawed character.

A FALSE PROPHET LACKS INTEGRITY: A false prophet has no integrity. He knows little or nothing of honor, virtue, or principle. He isn't honest or upright. He is not righteous in God's eyes, only self-righteous in his own.

A FALSE PROPHET PROMOTES SELF: A false prophet is also self-promoting. He is not interested in speaking God's word but only in speaking his own. He is not interested in building God's kingdom but only in building his own empire. Therefore, he does not lead people to God but to himself.

Outwardly his manner may seem godly and obedient, but inwardly, he serves only self, other men, or the enemy. He does not magnify and exalt the Lord. He does not prepare the way of the Lord. He is

A false prophet is self promoting.

the total antithesis of the prophetic ministry of John the Baptist. Instead of shining as a lamp to show the way to Christ (*John 5:35*), a false prophet shines to light his own way—or that of the antichrist. Rather than making Christ manifest and revealing Him to God's people (*John 1:31*), a false prophet reveals and enthrones himself.

A FALSE PROPHET COMPROMISES: It is also obvious that a false prophet compromises. He will speak any word if the price is right, but he will refuse to speak a word from God if it will cost him too much. He is willing to compromise God, the Scriptures, his honor and his integrity for the sake of a false ministry. That's a high price for nothing.

A FALSE PROPHET WON'T ENDURE: Often what prophets say is not well received. Sometimes the going gets rough. While a true prophet will stay and endure the slings and arrows of irate saints until the things of God come to pass, a false prophet is off at the first hint of opposition. While a true prophet is one of the first to engage the enemy in battle, a false prophet is one of the first to leave the scene of battle. He is usually long gone before the smoke clears.

A FALSE PROPHET IS REBELLIOUS: There is at least one more description of a false prophet. It encompasses all the other flaws and yet adds a new dimension and clarity to the understanding of his dark nature. As we learned in the previous chapter, a true prophet acts under the direction and authority of God *(John 12:49)*. A false prophet has no authority from God and therefore speaks on his own *(Jeremiah 23:21)*. This means that a primary character trait of a false prophet is not revelation but rebellion.

False prophets walk in and teach rebellion. Their lies, deception, and manipulation are evil fruit from an evil tree. Since rebellion is as the sin of witchcraft *(1 Samuel 15:23)*, this is a far place from the glories of the courts of heaven.

Scripture is clear in its warning against those who encourage rebellion against God:

> *Send to all those in captivity, saying, "Thus says the LORD concerning Shemaiah the Nehelamite: Because Shemaiah has prophesied to you, and I have not sent him, and he has caused you to trust in a lie, therefore thus says the LORD: 'Behold, I will punish Shemaiah the Nehelamite and his family: he shall not have anyone to dwell among this, nor shall he see the good that I will do for My people,'" says the LORD, "because he has taught rebellion against the LORD." Jeremiah 29:31-32 (NKJV)*

WHAT DOES A FALSE PROPHET DO?

As they differ in character, true and false prophets also differ in ministry.

A FALSE PROPHET DOES NOT SPEAK IN GOD'S NAME:
A true prophet is one who receives an understanding of
a word or the will of God and then speaks that forth as
God's legitimate spokesman. A false prophet does not. He
has not been in the courts of heaven and has not received
revelation from God. Therefore, whatever he speaks is
not by the command of God or in His name.

The true prophet derives his authority from the Godhead and from the Word. A false prophet does not. Since
he was not given his office by Jesus, his work is neither
guided nor inspired by the Holy Spirit. Rather, he himself,
another man, or Satan has called the false prophet to his
work, and the word he speaks reflects this source.

Additionally, false prophets feel that *their* word is su-
perior to *the Word* and therefore place themselves outside the authority of the written Word. Although heard
saying the right things about submission to the Word and
publicly doing things that look like they are under its rule,
in reality they are in open defiance to the final authority of
the inerrant Word of God. They actually resist rather than
receive authority from His Word.

A FALSE PROPHET LEADS PEOPLE AWAY FROM GOD:
A true prophet's goals are to motivate, restore, and guide.
A false prophet therefore will do contrary things. Rather
than stirring up truth, he will let error lie and caution saints
to do nothing to correct it. Rather than restore, revive, or
refresh, he neglects, opposes, and undermines. Rather
than lead sheep to God, he leads them away from Him.

LEVELS OF FALSE PROPHECY

1. THE FALSE MINISTER OF THE GRACE OF PROPHECY: Just as there are three levels of true prophets, there are three groups or stages of false prophets. The first false prophet is innocent, immature, and unknowledgeable, and yet the things he does and says harm the body of Christ. For example, this is the saint who hears an occasional word from God but is too frightened or unsure of himself to speak it forth, thus robbing the Church of a holy blessing. Or, it is the saint who has not been taught the difference between his grace level of prophesying, the ministry gift of prophecy given by the Holy Spirit, and the ascension gift of prophet given by Jesus. This saint, in ignorance or perhaps to ease the pressures of an insistent pastor, unintentionally steps over the boundaries of his prophetic grace and, without being called to either the ministry gift of prophecy or the office of prophet, takes on the work of a full-fledged prophet. He is heard rebuking and predicting, but there is no anointing on his work. He wonders why there is little, if any, fruit in his work and why people look at him funny.

2. THE FALSE MINISTER OF THE MINISTRY GIFT OF PROPHECY: The second and deeper level of error in the ministry of false prophecy are the agents of self or flesh. Some of these are the ignorant. Untaught, untrained, and often uncorrected by their local Church leaders, yet they are allowed to speak forth. Others are purposeful invaders of lives who know that the words they speak are not from God, but they deliver them anyway.

These false ministers often start with a desire to please someone else. They understand what a person wants to hear and "prophesy" that to them. Or, out of the unhealed wounds of their past, they speak forth a word from their own mind, heart, or emotions, hoping it will help another. This is ministry of the flesh, not the ministry of the Holy Spirit.

Often at this level of the prophetic, false prophecy starts with the desire to raise self. There are many would-be prophets running around the body of Christ speaking all manner of words in His name whose goals, hidden or obvious, are simply to be seen and heard. They don't know or care that since God didn't raise them up in the prophetic ministry, He will not honor them as such. Of them, the Lord says, *"I have not sent these prophets, yet they ran. I have not spoken to them, yet they prophesied"* (Jeremiah 23:21 NKJV).

If one claiming the ministry gift of prophecy has not been raised up by God, then he has not been invited by God into the counsels of heaven. As a consequence, he does not receive revelation of the will of God (illumination) nor the direction to speak that will through the Holy Spirit (inspiration). The results of these lapses are obvious.

When a false prophet utters a word that he infers is a message from God, he only assumes to know the will of God. He says what he thinks God thinks or proclaims what he thinks God would have said had he been with God to really know. Or, he generalizes a divine word given to him personally and speaks it out as direction for another or for his local Church. In essence, he is revealing his own will or, at best, guessing at God's. Then to authenticate the false or lend an air of the divine to the all too human, he slaps on a "thus sayeth the Lord" which deceives many.

3. THE FALSE PROPHET: Far beyond the scope of those who are innocent but harmful false "prophets" or the self-proclaimed and self-raised voices of flesh are the deliberately counterfeit agents of Satan. In the extreme, a false prophet will not speak on his own behalf, but be a representative of the enemy. He will not speak for God but for Satan *(Revelations 16:13-14)*.

True prophecy is the result of the Holy Spirit revealing God to man *(Ephesians 3:5; 2 Peter 1:21)*. **A reprobate prophet is an agent of Satan.** The Lord speaks through mouths of holy prophets *(Luke 1:70)*. But men who profane the things of God turn holiness into unholiness. They would switch masters and allow themselves to be used by an unholy spirit to speak to God's children. This offense is much more serious than bumbling because of inexperience or committing error through expressions of uncrucified flesh. It is consorting with the enemy. It is willfully being used as a tool of evil. It is anathema to God. Those engaged in such evil should hear and heed the warnings of the living Lord:

> And the word of the Lord came to me, saying, "Son of man, prophesy against the prophets of Israel

who prophesy, and say to those who prophesy out of their own heart, 'Hear the word of the LORD!'" Thus says the Lord GOD: "Woe to the foolish prophets, who follow their own spirit and have seen nothing!" Ezekiel 13:1-3 (NKJV)

They have envisioned futility and false divination, saying, "Thus says the LORD!" But the LORD has not sent them; yet they hope that the word may be confirmed. Have you not seen a futile vision, and have you not spoken false divination? You say, "The LORD says," but I have not spoken. Therefore thus says the Lord GOD: "Because you have spoken nonsense and envisioned lies, therefore I am indeed against you," says the Lord GOD. "My hand will be against the prophets who envision futility and who divine lies; they shall not be in the assembly of My people, nor be written in the record of the house of Israel, nor shall they enter into the land of Israel. Then you shall know that I am the Lord GOD." Ezekiel 13:6-9 (NKJV)

WARNING: THE SIGNS OF A FALSE PROPHET

FALSE PROPHETS PRESUME: False prophets do not acknowledge that Jesus, the Truth (*John 14:6*), can have no part of a lie. They operate on the premise that claiming something to be true will automatically make it true (*Ezekiel 23:6-7*). They do not acknowledge that a prophetic word stands true or false as it is given. If it is true, adding God's name to it won't make it more true. If it is false, adding God's name to it will never make it come true. However, it will make the one crediting God's name with error a blasphemer, for it is implying that God, not the false prophet, is a liar.

A FALSE PROPHET MANIPULATES: He will heighten the folly of his actions by speaking that which he has not heard from God hoping to make God act on that which was spoken "in His name." Especially if he has spoken his false word publicly, a false prophet will try to force God to honor it in order to make the false one look good. How many times has the untrue utterance, "You're healed, sister!" ended in a deathbed experience? This tragic occurrence belatedly exposes the false prophet's false word for the lie that it was. Sadly, it often leads those who have been wounded by the lie to doubt God rather than the false prophet.

Jesus had some not too complimentary things to say about the practices of false prophets. Specifically addressing the problems of presumption (or speaking a word from the prophet's heart) and manipulation (or attempting to coerce God into bringing it to pass), He warned:

Many will say to Me on that day, "Lord, Lord, have we not prophesied in Your name, and driven out demons in Your name, and done many mighty works in Your name?" and then I will say to them openly (publicly), "I never knew you; depart from me, you who act wickedly [disregarding My commands]."
Matthew 7:22-23 (TAB)

A FALSE PROPHET CHANGES SCRIPTURE: False prophets are running rampant through the body of Christ pro

False prophets change God's Word to their word. claiming a false word. They claim their private, ungodly revelations are based on Scripture when in reality they are not. They build empires on error. They add to and take from the one true Word. Their private word does not reveal or agree with God's whole Word. False prophets may begin in truth, but they soon deviate into falsehood. By one little but devious twist of a phrase, by the substitution of a different preposition, or by the deliberate and consistent misquoting of Scripture, a false prophet changes the true Word and leads the Church astray.

Undiscerning saints who believe that these false words that are true fall prey to the false prophet. Rather than following such a one, they should run from him. If a false prophet persists in proclaiming error, he should be disciplined by the Church.

A false prophet acts in rebellion. His lies, deception, and manipulation are evil fruit from an evil tree. They are manifestations of rebellion. Rebellion is as the sin of witchcraft (*1 Samuel 15:23*). This is a far place from the glories of the courts of heaven.

WARNING: A FALSE PROPHET USES SPURIOUS METHODS

Since function and character differ drastically between true prophet and false, it surely is no surprise to find out that methods used by true and false prophets are not the same either. A true prophet exhorts and builds; he reveals error by forth-telling; he reveals truth by foretelling. A false prophet causes error, and he hides truth. He does these things in nefarious ways.

A FALSE PROPHET MINISTERS THROUGH EMOTION: False prophets often use anger as a method of prophecy. Neither expressing God's holy anger nor caring that his outbursts cause the Father's house to be profaned, a false prophet will lash out in human anger at human targets.

False prophets draw people through the soul, not the spirit.

He uses human and unholy anger to target someone or something and that same anger to send countless missiles of destruction toward the person or the situation at which he is angry. He shouts a message that he says is of the Lord but which, in reality, is merely expressing his own ire, enmity, and hatred. Since he is out of right relationship with God because of bitterness, lack of forgiveness, resentment, or anger, he reveals that anger in his messages and then blasphemes God by blaming Him for it.

A FALSE PROPHET SPEAKS LIES: (*Ezekiel 13:6-9; 2 Chronicles 18:21*). In building for self or for Satan, a false prophet is not content with and often does not know the truth. A true prophet is inspired by the Spirit of Truth; a false one is not. Not to be dissuaded from speaking something in order to keep the attention on himself, a false prophet spews forth lies.

A FALSE PROPHET DECEIVES: His whole goal in uttering false prophecy is to promote himself and his ministry or Satan and his kingdom. Dressed as a sheep, the false prophet is in reality a devouring wolf *(Matthew 7:15)*. He twists words and facts to his advantage. He raises up his own body or army and attempts to pull it out of the true Church. This unscrupulous one preys on unsuspecting lambs, feeds them with poisonous words, leads them away from the main flock, and eventually imprisons them in error. The false prophet becomes not their leader but their warden *(Jeremiah 23:17)*. Out of such, cults are born. In these ways, saints are not led to the wonders of God but to the wickedness of man. They are not led to holiness but are constantly exposed to the unholy.

A FALSE PROPHET SEEKS POWER: Seeking to have power and the authority to manifest gifts and miracles, a false prophet may approach those with true power and gifts and use underhanded means in an attempt to get those things for himself.

> A false prophet seeks power for personal gain and fame.

Concerning the lust for power, the Word tells us of a man named Bar-Jesus:

Now when they had gone through the island to Pa-phos, they found a certain sorcerer, a false prophet, a Jew whose name was Bar-Jesus, who was with the proconsul, Sergius Paulus, an intelligent man. This man called for Barnabas and Saul and sought to hear the word of God. But Elymas the sorcerer (for so his name is translated) withstood them, seeking to turn the proconsul away from the faith. Then Saul, who also is called Paul, filled with the Holy Spirit, looked intently at him and said, "O full of all deceit and all fraud, you son of the devil, you enemy of all righteousness, will you not cease perverting the straight ways of the Lord?" Acts 13:6-10 (NKJV)

Bar-Jesus was specifically described as a false prophet. To acquire stature and importance in the eyes of men he had inveigled his way into fellowship with a proconsul and then gained power and influence both with him and through him. That the power he was exerting was evil and that it was meant to manipulate the proconsul to do things Bar-Jesus' way is quite obvious as the rest of the story is revealed.

One day the proconsul called Barnabas and Paul, ambassadors of truth, to himself. Bar-Jesus knew that if the proconsul heard the truth, he would recognize Bar-Jesus' words as the lies they were and turn away from him. Therefore, in desperation, Bar-Jesus did all he could to keep the proconsul from the apostles.

But truth won out, and manipulation was defeated. Bar-Jesus was soundly rebuked, and he lost his power and influence over the proconsul.

In another example of the Lord exposing the heart of a false prophet, Acts 8:9-20 tells the story of a man named Simon who claimed that he was a rather extraordinary, amazing person (*Acts 8:9*). It would seem that this claim to fame was based on his ability to practice magic (*Acts 8:9*). Through his evil practices, he drew men to himself, not to God, and gloried in the attention he received (*Acts 8:19*).

When the gospel message reached Samaria, Simon, along with many others, was astonished, believed, and was baptized (*Acts 8:13*). Soon Simon was amazed for another reason: this master of magic saw the truth. He saw signs and wonders being honestly and powerfully performed by true men of God: Phillip (*Acts 8:13*), Peter, and John (*Acts 8:17-18*). What glorious, wonderful miracles they must have been to amaze a magician!

Rather than submit to God, Simon resorted to evil. He had received salvation, but he would not yield to sanctification. He wouldn't alter his evil ways or allow God's holiness to change him. He just wanted holy power added onto his own unholy magic. Like all false prophets, he wanted to use the power of God to shine before men. He wanted to have holy power to further amaze people and draw them to himself.

Deceitfully he approached the apostles: *"Now when Simon saw that through the laying on of the apostle's hands the Holy Spirit was given, he offered them money, saying, 'Give me this power also, that anyone on whom I lay hands may receive the Holy Spirit'"* (Acts 8:18-19 NKJV).

Simon placed a price on the gift of God. Evilly coveting what others rightfully had, he tried to buy for himself the gift and power of God. Seeing through his lies, Peter said, *"Your money perish with you, because you thought that the gift of God could be purchased with money!"* (Acts 8:20 NKJV).

THE FRUIT OF FALSE PROPHETS

The results of this infiltration of evil have been staggering to the Church. It is obvious that if both the message and messenger have gone awry, the fruit will be rotten too.

CONFUSION: At the very least, false prophecy brings confusion to the Church. An assembly of God is made up of saints who are at all levels of maturity and therefore at all levels of susceptibility or discernment. When false prophecy is uttered and not corrected, the young in the Lord do not know what to believe. Particularly if it is the leadership in the local Church that is speaking error or proclaiming those things that do not agree with what God has truly whispered into a heart, the young in Christ are caught in the middle. If saints of all ages are not aware that a prophetic word should draw them to inquire about it from God or confirm what He has

False prophecy brings confusion.

already spoken to them, they may be led to do some fool-ish things. The end result is that they may walk in confu-sion for years and never be an effective member of the body of Christ.

CHAOS: After confusion comes chaos. On a wider scale, involving more of the body and bringing even more

Confusion leads to chaos.

damaging results, false words lead to chaos. God speaks one Word; the false prophets report another. The true sons of God go one way; the gullible go another. The result is a milling mass of people going nowhere.

SEDUCTION: Then seduction creeps in (Ezekiel 13:10). In trying to correct the situation, God may send a word of

Chaos leads to seduction.

admonition through a true prophet. This may lead some to turn from their corrector. Or, God may allow a false prophetic word to be spoken to test the saints and to determine those who will serve only him (Deuteronomy 13:1-3). However some of the saints may not understand this to be the warning that it is, fall for the false signs and stride even farther away from Him. If saints don't have the ears or the heart to hear truth, they are susceptible to hear the lie. They are gradually se-duced into the camp of the enemy.

APOSTASY: If seduction is planted, apostasy will

Seduction leads to apostasy.

grow. False prophecy leads peo-ple away from God. If introduced into the Church, it brings that

Church into error *(Lamentations 2:9)*. If already in the Church, it allows error to deepen *(Lamentations 2:14)*. In no case does false prophecy honor or promote God.

DESTRUCTION: Finally, false prophecy, in its worst role, destroys a Church. A Church with no vision will fall into ritual and die *(Proverbs 29:18)*. So also a Church with

False prophecy destroys a Church.

false vision will perish. The Word is very clear in the picture it paints that the end of that Church which does not confront and stop evil is annihilation. It specifically states that devouring wolves (false prophets) will eat the sheep *(Matthew 7:15)*. Even more graphic are the words of *Ezekiel: 22:25-28 (TAB)*:

> *There is a conspiracy of [Israel's false] prophets in the midst of her, like a roaring lion tearing the prey; they have devoured human lives; they have taken [in their greed] treasure and precious things; they have made many widows in the midst of her. Her priests have done violence to My law and have profaned My holy things. They have made no distinction between the sacred and the secular, neither have they taught people the difference between the unclean and the clean, and have hid their eyes from My Sabbaths, and I am profaned among them. Her princes in the midst of her are like wolves rending and devouring the prey, shedding blood and destroying lives to get dishonest gain. And her prophets have daubed for them with whitewash, seeing false visions and divining lies to them, saying, Thus says the Lord God, when the Lord has not spoken.*

False prophets do not build God's Church. They destroy it! They do not lead the saints away from error but into error. As there is a ruinous end to a Church who hears and heeds false words, there is also a bad ending for the false prophet himself: *"But the prophet who presumes to speak a word in my name, which I have not commanded him to speak, or who speaks in the name of other gods, that prophet shall die"* (Deuteronomy 18:20 NKJV).

OUR RESPONSE TO THE FALSE PROPHET

By now it should be obvious that there is a major problem in the Church concerning false prophecy. What may not be so clear is that each of us, not just our pastors, has an obligation before God to do something about the problem. The battle of truth versus falsehood must be confronted, fought, and won. It is up to every saint to enlist as a soldier, take his place in God's army, and stand.

DISCERN: To refute false prophecy, the first thing a saint must do is to discern. As the apostle John warns us: *"Beloved, do not believe every spirit, but test the spirits, whether they are of God; because many false prophets have gone out into the world"* (1 John 4:1 NKJV).

All spirits are not godly ones. All spirits are not the Holy Spirit. Individually and as a people of God, we need to know the source of any word we hear. We need to ascertain who spoke to the one speaking to us. True prophets speak for God; the false do not. It is specifically the job and joy of saints to know His voice.

JUDGE THE WORD: Before accepting or walking in any prophetic word, it is necessary for each saint to judge any word given to him or her privately. It is also necessary for the leadership of the Church to judge any word given to the body of Christ publicly (*1 Corinthians 14:29*). In so doing, care must be taken to judge both the content of the word spoken and the spirit behind the word. Any word judged as right or true should be accepted and acted on; any incorrect word should be rejected and ignored.

There are specific ways to judge the authenticity of prophecy. The first way is to be sure that a prophetic word lines up with Scripture. God will not contradict His written Word by a spoken word. Any prophetic word must agree with the

Test: Does the prophecy line up with Scripture?

doctrine and principles set forth in Scripture or it is not a true prophetic word. It is impossible to overemphasize the preeminence and authority of *the* Word as the judge of *a* word. Since the Word is complete, inerrant, and unchanging and man's words are not, saints must use His Word as their only standard or judge.

A second test as to the truth of a prophetic word is to verify whether or not it comes to pass. While in some unique instances, God will allow the words of a false prophet to come to pass in order to test men (*Deuteronomy 13:1-3*), His Word also says:

> *Declaring the end from the beginning, and from ancient times things that are not yet done, saying, "My*

*counsel shall stand, and I will do all My pleasure, call-
ing a bird of prey from the east, the man who executes My counsel, from a far country. Indeed I have
spoken it; I will also bring it to pass; I have purposed
it; I will also do it." Isaiah 46:10-11 (NKJV)*

*And if you say in your heart, "How shall we know
the word which the LORD has not spoken?"—when
a prophet speaks in the name of the LORD, if the
thing does not happen or come to pass, that is the
thing which the Lord has not spoken; the prophet
has spoken it presumptuously; you shall not be
afraid of him. Deuteronomy 18:21-22 (NKJV)*

Understand that God moves in His own time and that
God watches over His Word to perform it *(Isaiah 55:11)*.

**Test: Does the
prophecy
come to pass?** He does not watch over error to
perform it. He does not watch over
man's or Satan's word to perform
it. If a false word is uttered, God will
not honor it. He will not perform it either to save face for
or to be manipulated by a false prophet. Thus, unless He
is testing His Church, a false word is a profitless (and
prophetless) word that will remain unfulfilled by God.

The Church is not the only place where any word of
prophecy should be judged. In the home it is the father
or husband who, as the head of the family, should hear
and weigh any word spoken to or about members of his
household. As he is responsible before God for his wife's
and children's welfare, he must judge any words prophet-

ically spoken to them. How many disastrous marriages, ungodly careers, and tragedies could have been prevented by testing prophecies?

In the Old Testament dispensation, leaven was often equated with sin and evil. During the Feast of Unleavened Bread, it was the father's job to take a candle and go through his whole house looking for leaven. If he found any, he was to put it out of his house. Today, saints need to heed this. How many twenty-first century households are in the dark because the father would not use his Light to discover the sin and evil of false prophecy that affected the members of his family and to throw it out of his house?

JUDGE THE MESSENGER: In addition to judging the message, each saint and the Church as a whole should judge the messenger. A young, immature saint just beginning to respond to the call to the prophetic can and will make mistakes in his presentation of the word. That doesn't make him a false prophet. Similarly, if one with the gift of prophecy has a peculiar way of presenting it, that doesn't make him a false prophet. However, the truly false one must have his word as well as his ways judged. From what spirit is the messenger receiving his messages?

In the early Church, the apostle Paul ran into a false messenger and he wasted no time in dealing with her. As Acts 16 recounts, while Paul and his team were on their way to prayer they met a slave girl whose so-called prophetic gift was a money-making scheme for her masters.

Following after Paul, she continuously cried out: *"These men are the servants of the Most High God who proclaim to us the way of salvation" (Acts 16:17 NKJV).*

Obeying the admonition in 1 Corinthians 14 to judge every word of prophecy, it is seen that her message was true. Paul and his team were indeed God's servants announcing the only path to relationship with Him. However, in complying with the command to judge the spirits (1 John 4:1), it is seen that the messenger was false. She was *"possessed with a spirit of divination" (Acts 16:16 NKJV).* Recognizing the unholy source of her words, Paul didn't allow her to go unchallenged. He turned to her and commanded the evil spirit to come out of her.

CORRECT ERROR: After judging and finding a message or the messenger to be false there are some things the Church should do to keep the ministry of the prophet honorable. One such thing is to correct error.

If a word of prophecy is found to be false, it should be corrected. If a messenger is found false, he or she should be corrected. If that same messenger is repeatedly found to be false yet persists in spreading error, he should be rebuked.

Publicly, it is the responsibility of the Church and its leadership to respond. Even if the bearer of a false message is a respected leader or a pastor, if he repeatedly speaks false words he must be stopped. 1 Timothy 5, in its directions for rebuking elders, gives a clear warning that no one in the body of Christ—and that includes its leaders—is above godly discipline if discipline is needed.

Privately, it is each saint's responsibility to act after receiving a questionable or false word. If he refutes a word spoken to him, he has an obligation to go to those with whom he disagrees. If he is stonewalled in his attempts to discover the truth, he should go to his Church leaders with questions and concerns.

Similarly, in the home, while all mature members of a family are to judge prophetic words spoken to them, it is the husband or father who bears the added responsibility to deal with a false prophet and his prophecy. Anyone not wanting to speak or repeat the words he has spoken to women or children to the head of the household is hiding something.

INSTRUCT THE CHURCH CONCERNING THE SPIRITUAL GIFTS AND THE PROPHETIC OFFICE: Another thing that the Church and its leaders must do to stop the flood of false prophecy is to instruct believers concerning the gifts of the Holy Spirit. Saints are not always taught to differentiate between a prophetic utterance and any other spoken gift of the Spirit. A false prophet exploits this ignorance; he leads saints to error because they do not realize that all words of revelation spoken at an assembly of saints are not prophetic words.

Words of knowledge or words of wisdom are also valid ministry gifts given to the Church by the Holy Spirit (*1 Corinthians 12:8*) but they are not always synonymous with the ministry gift of prophecy. Nor are they an alternative to exercising the ascension gift of prophet.

Words of knowledge, words of wisdom, and prophecy, while closely allied, are three separate gifts. They are for separate needs and functions, and they produce different results. Yet, so often when someone expresses any one of these gifts, it is automatically labeled as a prophetic word. This lack of teaching concerning the differences between the gifts and prophetic office, the improper expression of ministry gifts, and the elevation of all revelatory words to the status of prophecy have hampered and hindered both the proper working of the Holy Spirit in His ministry among people and the effective working of Jesus in raising up the true prophets of God.

WARN FALSE PROPHETS: Finally, as a means of correcting false prophecy, the Word says to prophesy against the false prophets.

> Son of man, prophesy against the prophets of Israel who prophesy, and say to those who prophesy out of their own heart, "Hear the word of the Lord!" Thus says the Lord GOD: "Woe to the foolish prophets, who follow their own spirit and have seen nothing!" Ezekiel 13:2-3 (NKJV)

They must be made to know that if they continue in their evil ways, they are in danger. It is God who said:

> My hand will be against the prophets who envision futility and who divine lies; they shall not be in the assembly of My people, nor be written in the record of the house of Israel, nor shall they enter into the land of Israel. Then you shall know that I am the

Lord GOD. Because, indeed, because they have My people, saying, "Peace!" when there is no peace— and one builds a boundary wall, and they plaster it with untempered mortar—say to those who plaster it with untempered mortar, that it will fall. There will be flooding, rain, and you, O great hailstones, shall fall; and a stormy wind shall tear it down. Surely, when the wall has fallen, will it not be said to you, "Where is the mortar with which you plastered it?" Therefore thus says the Lord GOD: "I will cause a stormy wind to break forth in My fury; and there shall be a flooding rain in My anger, and great hailstones in fury to consume it. So I will break down the wall you have plastered with untempered mortar, and bring it down to the ground, so that its foundation will be uncovered; it will fall, and you shall be consumed in the midst of it. Then you shall know that I am the LORD. Thus will I accomplish My wrath on the wall and on those who have plastered it with untempered mortar, and I will say to you, "The wall is no more, nor those who plastered it, that is the prophets...." Ezekiel 13:9-16 (NKJV)

These words about false prophets may sound harsh to some. However, in order to allow true prophets to do the job God sends them to do, the false prophets must be exposed and rejected. Unfortunately, there are some who reject the true prophets instead. Although the true Church is even now being encircled by the rebellious who cry out to seers, *"'See not!' and to prophets, 'Prophesy* not!'" (Isaiah 30:10 TAB), yet God's Word says that quenching, suppressing, or denying true prophecy is contrary to His will.

Rather than allowing His saints to wander in the darkness of "prophecy not," the Lord has said, "I send you prophets...." (Matthew 23:34 NKJV). And, through Peter, He admonishes us: "We also have the prophetic word made more sure, which you do well to heed as a light that shines in a dark place, until the day dawns and the morning star rises in your hearts" (2 Peter 1:19 NKJV).

The ministry of prophets and prophecy is the will of God for His Church—but only the true, not the false.

PROPHETS

	TRUE PROPHETS	FALSE PROPHETS
CHARACTER:	• people of integrity • promote God • will not compromise truth • endure hardship • are submitted to God	• lack integrity and honor • promote themselves • compromise truth • won't endure — leave the scene of battle • are rebellious against God
PURPOSE:	• hear a word from God and speak it forth in a way, place, and time of His choosing • lead people to God	• do not hear from God and so speak from self or from an unholy spirit • lead people away from God

LEVELS:	THE GRACE: those who are occasionally asked by God to share something in the local church that He has revealed to them	• the inexperienced who refuse to speak forth a word from God or who speak forth a word not from God
	THE MINISTRY: those who are obedient to speak that which God reveals and who become increasingly more accurate and assured as they do so in their local Church and community	• the agents of self who speak for themselves in an effort to build their own name and gain some fame; those who take on the functions of a prophet
	THE PROPHET: those who hear the word of God and honorably speak it forth; those who are God's mouthpiece in a local, community or worldwide arena	• the agents of Satan who try to destroy the Church by speaking a false word to the Church
METHOD:	• do not take advantage of, take liberties with, exploit, or use God • do not distort, alter, change, tamper with or misrepresent God's word • speak truth • are honest • give glory to god • stay within ministry boundaries	• presume • manipulate • speak lies • deceive • seek personal power • take on unauthorized expansion of ministry

EVANGELISTS: THE TRUE

"Go into all the world and preach the gospel to every creature." Mark 16:16 (NKJV)

The gift of evangelist is the third ascension gift given to the body of Christ by Jesus (*Ephesians 4:11*). After the apostles and prophets have laid the foundation of the Church and have engaged themselves in building and directing it, it is time for the evangelists to do their work.

Taken from the Greek, the word for evangelist is *euaggelistes*. It means one who proclaims the good news. The words good news are also from a Greek word, *euaggelion*, and mean "the message of the kingdom of God and the salvation of man through the blood of Jesus Christ." From *euaggelistes* and *euaggelion*, it is easy to see how closely related the man and the ministry, the messenger and the message, the evangelist and the pronouncement of the good news really are.

By way of definition then, an evangelist is one who proclaims the gospel of salvation. If he is an anointed vessel of God, the results of his message are that souls are saved, new saints are baptized (*Acts 8:6,12*), and the Church continuously grows.

In order to do his work successfully, an evangelist must thoroughly understand the message he is presenting. He must know and be able to express what the gospel of the kingdom of God is, that it is at hand, and that salvation into the kingdom comes only through the blood of Jesus Christ. He must be clearly able to explain that man does not have to establish God's kingdom; God already has. Nor does he have to overcome the world; Jesus already has.

It was John the Baptist, followed by Jesus Christ Himself, who introduced the kingdom of God into an unbelieving world (*Matthew 3:2; 4:17*). It was to this kingdom, God's kingdom and no other, that John and Jesus drew people. From them and from Scripture several truths about the kingdom of God can be learned:

- The kingdom of God is not the perfection of the physical kingdom of humans on earth; it is a spiritual kingdom found in the hearts of believers (*John 18:36*).
- The kingdom of God is not the attempt by people to cleanse soul or body of sin or to make themselves righteous through human works of flesh; it is Jesus cleansing and setting aright a person's spirit by the power of His Holy Spirit.
- The kingdom of God is not a temporal one; it is an eternal one.

Of the greatest importance for all in the first century and all in the twenty-first century to understand, the kingdom of God is a sovereign one which rules over all others. The prophet Daniel tells us about this kingdom:

"And in the days of these kings the God of heaven will set up a kingdom which shall never be destroyed; and the kingdom shall not be left to other people; it shall break in pieces and consume all these kingdoms, and it shall stand forever" (Daniel 2:44 NKJV).

In addition to knowing about the kingdom, evangelists must comprehend the King. The existence of a kingdom implies the need for a king. The kingdom of God is ruled by King Jesus. The kingdom of God was first established by God and then given to Jesus to rule.

I was watching in the night visions, and behold, One like the Son of Man, coming with the clouds of heaven! He came to the Ancient of Days, and they brought Him near before Him. Then to Him was given dominion and glory and a kingdom, that all peoples, nations, and languages should serve Him. His dominion is an everlasting dominion, which shall not pass away. And His kingdom the one which shall not be destroyed.   Daniel 7:13-14 (NKJV)

After learning about God's kingdom and King, evangelists must take their cue from the angel Gabriel and fulfill their evangelistic calling by announcing them to all mankind. In Luke 1:31-33 (NKJV) Gabriel says:

And behold, you will conceive in your womb and bring forth a Son, and shall call His name JESUS. He will be great, and will be called the Son of the Highest; and the Lord God will give Him the throne of

His father David. And He will reign over the house of Jacob forever, and of His kingdom there will be no end.

It is the job of evangelists to preach the kingdom of God. They must announce that this spiritual, eternal kingdom has begun on earth within the hearts of believers. They must proclaim that the way into this kingdom is through Jesus, the Savior. They must announce that while yet immature, this kingdom shall soon be complete when the King of kings comes to claim His kingdom, His throne, and His people: *"Then the seventh angel sounded: And there were loud voices in heaven, saying, 'The kingdoms of this world have become the kingdoms of our Lord and of His Christ, and He shall reign forever and ever!'"* (Revelations 11:15 NKJV).

GOOD CHARACTER

A TRUE EVANGELIST IS OTHER-ORIENTED: In order to do his work successfully, an evangelist must be a person of character. He must be selfless. Like the prophet, one of his strongest character traits is self-denial. Often up all night or constantly on the road in strange and sometimes dangerous places, he denies himself human comforts in order to fulfill his calling. Rather than in any way drawing attention to self, he is forever pointing to Jesus.

A TRUE EVANGELIST IS EARNEST: Another character trait of a true evangelist is earnestness. He in no way embodies the nonchalant, laid-back minister with the easy gospel that is sometimes the modern caricature of the true evangelistic calling. Rather, he is a man who constantly and zealously presents his salvation message because he knows that in every passing moment a soul can be saved or lost. To him, salvation is not a laughing matter but one with life or death consequences.

WHAT DOES AN EVANGELIST DO?

Just as an evangelist has a specific job to do and is marked with certain character traits, he also has an effective method for fulfilling his mission. His methods, while different from those of ministers in other offices, help him to function in his particular calling.

A TRUE EVANGELIST IS OUT, NOT IN: A true evangelist knows that there is no point in presenting a message of salvation to those already saved; his message and his ministry are to the unsaved. He is therefore aware that if a Church is a gathering of the saved, the majority of his work is to be done outside the Church in his local community or in the world. In order to work effectively, in order to reach the unsaved, the evangelist must leave the Church (physically, not spiritually) and go out where the unsaved are found.

An evangelist does not, indeed cannot, evangelize the evangelized. His ministry is to those who do not know the Lord, not to those who do. His ministry is not to those who have been blessed by salvation through the blood of Jesus but to those who have not.

An evangelist has a deep hunger and thirst for souls. His heart cries out over the plight of the unsaved. All that is within him wants—needs—to see the hunger, the thirst, and the emptiness in unsaved souls filled by Jesus. Since his own need to see souls saved cannot be met among the saved, he goes to where the need is. At any time of day or night, in any place (coffee house, bar, hospital, prison) an evangelist is among the unsaved presenting the gospel of Jesus Christ. He goes out to lead them in.

A TRUE EVANGELIST'S WEAPON IS THE WORD OF GOD: While among the unsaved, the true evangelist has but one job. Since, with all his heart, he wants to see sinners become saints, he must fire volleys of truth into unbelieving hearts. To do so, an evangelist's chief weapon is the infallible Word of God. Only in the Word is the gospel message contained. Only in the Word, is the salvation message explained.

Specifically from the Word, the evangelist must preach Jesus (Acts 8:5). It is the privilege and joy of the evangelist to introduce the most important person in the Word, Jesus, and the most important part of the Word, the message of salvation through Him alone.

After explaining to sinners that the first Adam, mankind's forefather, fell into sin and by that sin he and all his descendants were separated from God, a true evangelist will show that the only way to be reunited with the Father is through the last Adam, God's Son. He will share that reconciliation with God can only come through the shed blood of Jesus, the perfect, sinless Passover Lamb. He will tell the unsaved that all sins were placed on Jesus who suffered, shed His blood, and died to atone for them, making forgiveness of sin and salvation available to all who would call upon the name of the Lord.

An evangelist makes it abundantly clear to the unsaved that salvation cannot come through works but through faith in the name of Jesus. It cannot come through error or heresy but through belief in the Word that perfectly preaches Jesus. It cannot come through ritual or religion but through living relationship with the living Lord. It cannot come through false gods or false ways but through the One True God and the only Way, Jesus.

This introduction of Jesus as the Savior and of His work at the cross as the means of salvation is the limit of the presentation of the gospel by anyone functioning as an evangelist. Since he realizes that a deeper presentation of the Word, while helpful and indeed essential to a saint, only serves to confuse those who are in need of salvation, an evangelist confines his message to the issues of Jesus and His kingdom, the cross, and forgiveness of sin. Other preaching and teaching, since it edifies the Church rather than saves souls, is left to those anointed to do so.

A TRUE EVANGELIST'S MINISTRY IS ACCOMPANIED BY SIGNS AND WONDERS: In order to effectively do all of this, in order to attract the unsaved so that the testimony of Jesus can be presented to them, an evangelist's ministry is often accompanied by signs and wonders. Through

the Holy Spirit an evangelist is empowered to do supernatural, godly works that the ungodly will notice and re

The ministry of evangelism is often accompanied by the miraculous.

spond to. True evangelists realize that these miracles do not save; they only serve as a drawing card for the introduction of the Savior, Jesus. True evangelists know that while miracles are mani-
festations of God's power, there is no salvation in the
miracles themselves. The power unto salvation is in the
Word, not in miraculous works.

> For I am not ashamed of the gospel (good news) of
> Christ; for it is God's power working unto salvation
> (for deliverance from eternal death) to every one
> who believes with a personal trust and a confident
> surrender and firm reliance, to the Jew first and also
> to the Greek. Romans 1:16 (TAB)

A TRUE EVANGELIST LEADS PEOPLE TO CHURCH: Finally, a true evangelist will see that new Christians understand that they are now a part of God's family and that
God's family is the Church. The evangelist will lead new
saints to God's Church (Acts 2:41). New lambs are not
left to wander alone in the world where wolves can isolate them and eat them alive. They are brought into and
added to the flock of God (Acts 16:5). They are carefully
placed under the care of a godly shepherd.

GOD'S FISHERMAN

It is easy to compare the work of an evangelist with that of a fisherman. A fisherman is one who desires to catch fish. From past experience, from news broadcast by word of mouth, or in a bold new venture, a fisherman knows where to go and when to go there in order to find fish. Carefully planning his foray, the fisherman will take into account the kind of fish he wants to catch, the waters they are found in, and even the weather conditions. He will carefully check his equipment to see that his lines, reels, rods, bait, clothing, food, and boat are set for the adventure. Then, he will go where the fish are, throw out his line, catch them, reel the fish in, and add them in growing numbers to his basket.

Just so, the work of an evangelist is to "catch" souls. He finds the unsaved where God tells him they will be, and he knows the best times to seek them there. Once he knows where he is going, he plans his campaign. He checks the conditions so he can effectively deal with any limitations of time, place, or weather. Then, going out to the unsaved rather than waiting for them to come to him, he drops his line into the water. Perhaps through the manifestation of a godly miracle as his bait, he lures them. It is, however, the hook or the gospel of Jesus Christ, that snags the unbeliever and holds him fast as he is brought in. Then the evangelist sees that his catch is added to the other fish in the basket, the saints in the kingdom of God or the Church.

LEVELS OF EVANGELISTS

As has been noted in studying the offices of apostles and prophets, there are different levels of ministry. This is also true of evangelism. Jesus commanded all disciples to *"go into all the world"* (*Matthew 28:19*), but only some of them were anointed with the ascension gift of apostle. The Holy Spirit desires that all minister in the local Church with a prophetic word (*1 Corinthians 14:5*), but only some are gifted as prophets. The same pattern holds true with evangelists. All God's people are enjoined to go and preach the gospel to every creature (*Mark 16:15*), but of these, Jesus chose only some to be His evangelists (*Ephesians 4:11*).

   1. THE GRACE OF EVANGELISM: Long before anyone can function in the office of evangelism, a saint must experience the grace of evangelism. He must allow himself to be occasionally used of God to share the good news and lead an unbeliever to Jesus for salvation. If he is faithful in the little, he may then be raised up and asked to function in more, the ministry gift of evangelism.

   2. THE MINISTRY GIFT OF EVANGELISM: The ministry of evangelism can be individual ministry on a broader scale or the inclusion into a group sent as an outreach from a local Church. For instance, teams might be sent into hospitals or prisons to spread the good news with the intention of saving the unsaved and adding to the Church. It is in this area, under the authority of and yet in the midst of the local body, that the manifestation of signs and wonders may begin to be evidenced in the saints walking in the ministry of evangelism.

One sign occasionally seen in an evangelist's work is miraculous healing. The ministry gifts of healings (1 Corinthians 12:9) are the manifestation of the healing power of the Holy Spirit through human vessels. They function in the local Church to maintain or to restore health in the body. When joined with evangelism, they are a means to draw the unsaved near to hear the healing message of Christ.

3. THE EVANGELIST: Finally, there is the ascension gift of the office of evangelist. An evangelist goes beyond the restrictions of both the grace or ministry gift of evangelism to proclaim salvation. He serves through a local Church, but he is not limited to service in the local body. He is authorized to go far beyond those boundaries and serve the universal Church as well. While the work of an evangelist does involve miracles and signs and wonders, one of which may be healings, his main thrust is not with the physical health or restoration of the bodies of the saved but with the spiritual health of the souls of the unsaved. His main ministry is speaking the good news of salvation to those who are dead in spirit.

HOW IS AN EVANGELIST CHOSEN?

By the request of Jesus Christ, it is the privilege of all saints to proclaim the good news of salvation from sin and the world of darkness into forgiveness and the kingdom of light at the local community level.

Just after He arose from the dead, Jesus met two disciples who were walking on the road to Emmaus. Heavy of heart and unaware that the "stranger" they were talking to was Jesus, they discussed the recent events in Jerusalem where Jesus had been crucified on a cross. In His mercy to them, "*....beginning at Moses and all the Prophets, He expounded to them in all the Scriptures the things concerning Himself*" (Luke 24:27 NKJV). When the two disciples returned to Jerusalem to share their story with the rest of the disciples, Jesus again drew near and stood in the midst of all of them. Proving that He was indeed Jesus, the crucified Savior, He declared that the things that had happened were to fulfill words written about Him in the Law of Moses, the Prophets, and the Psalms. He then explained why all these things had happened: "*Thus it is written, and thus it was necessary for the Christ to suffer and to rise from the dead the third day, and that repentance and remission of sins should be preached in His name to all nations, beginning at Jerusalem*" (Luke 24:46-47 NKJV).

And then He told the disciples why they were eligible to tell His story: "*....you are witnesses of these things*" (Luke 24:48 NKJV).

Those disciples of yesterday are His disciples today. Each saint who understands Jesus' sacrifice and the victory of the cross are deputized to enlighten those who don't.

Yet, there is more. Out of the many, Jesus has chosen some to be evangelists or those with the calling, anointing, and appointment to be those who tell His good news on a world-wide stage: *"And He Himself gave some to be....evangelists...."* (Ephesians 4:11 NKJV).

JESUS, THE EVANGELIST

As with the other ascension gifts, the perfect example of an evangelist and the role model for all evangelists is Jesus.

Early in His ministry, Jesus was seen as an evangelist. After His miraculous birth, after John prepared His way, after His baptism by the Holy Spirit and His subsequent temptation in the wilderness by the enemy, Jesus went to the region of Galilee. His reason for doing so reveals His heart of evangelism.

> *The people who sat (dwelt enveloped) in darkness have seen a great Light, and for those who sat in the land and shadow of death Light has dawned. From that time Jesus began to preach, crying out, "Repent—that is, change your mind for the better, heartily amend your ways, with abhorrence of your past sins—for the kingdom of heaven is at hand."* Matthew 4:16-17 (TAB)

Then, walking in the office of evangelist and declaring God's kingdom, Jesus began to call men unto Himself. As He walked near the Sea of Galilee, He saw two brothers, Simon and Andrew, casting a net into the sea. He said to them, *"Come after Me [as disciples]—letting Me be your Guide, follow Me—and I will make you fishers of men"* (Matthew 4:19 TAB). They did so. Soon, Jesus saw two more brothers, James and John, mending nets in a ship with their father. Again, the call rang out, and they too left ship and family and joined Jesus *(Matthew 4:21-22).*

The Word further says that Jesus preached the gospel of the kingdom and, as He did so, miracles accompanied His message: diseases were healed, demons were cast out, and great multitudes were drawn to Him *(Matthew 4:23; 6:24-25)*. He preached to the unsaved wherever He found them. Synagogues, mountainsides, seashores, and private homes *(Matthew 4:1,18,23; Luke 19:4-8)* all became theaters for the presentation of the good news. He brought the sinner-turned-saint into the body now called His Church.

FIRST CENTURY EVANGELISTS

It is obvious that some of the Lord's disciples, such as Andrew and Philip, learned their evangelistic lessons well. Exhibiting a grace of evangelism, they both brought others to Christ *(John 1:40-42, 44-46)*. The apostle Paul indicates that Timothy had a ministry of evangelism *(2 Timothy 4:5)*. However, there is one who most stands out as a man functioning in the office of the evangelist. His name is Phillip.

We meet Phillip (not the same man as the apostle) in the book of Acts. He is described as a man of honest rapport who was filled with the Holy Spirit and wisdom *(Acts 6:3)*. He was selected to serve as a deacon in the Church in Jerusalem *(Acts 6:5)*. Soon after the death of Stephen, persecution broke out in the Church. As a result, believers were scattered far and wide. Rather than being cowed by the enemy, they, in great faith, used the opportunity as a chance to spread the gospel wherever they went (Acts 8:4).

Phillip went to Samaria and there he preached Christ to the unsaved (Acts 8:5). Accompanying his works were miracles, healings, and deliverances (Acts 8:6-7). The result of his work is that sinners became saints and were baptized (Acts 8:12).

In his work, Phillip confined his message to salvation through Jesus Christ. He did not wander off topic to preach other godly but non-evangelistic messages. This can be seen in that as soon as the Church in Jerusalem heard that some in Samaria had been saved, Peter and John were sent to them (Acts 8:14). It had been Phillip's job to see the unsaved brought into right relationship with the Father; it was the job of others to lay the foundation for the Church among the new saints, to preach the doctrines of God, and then build and direct the new work.

TWENTY-FIRST CENTURY EVANGELISTS

Unlike the argument that surrounds the offices of apostles and prophets, today's Church acknowledges the need for evangelists. Those who are willing to sacrifice themselves in order to promote God are badly needed in the Church.

The job of evangelists today is still to preach Jesus. They must still sow the Seed into the sometimes hardened soil of human hearts. This Seed that has fallen into the ground and died (John 12:24) has also sprung up to new life *(Matthew 28:6; Luke 24:7)*. This Seed, if accepted by man, has the potential to bring that same resurrection Life into the deadened spirit of every unbeliever and into the heart of every person. This Seed, who is Jesus, can raise the dead, sinful human spirit into new resurrected life. This is what Jesus meant when He said: *"You must be born again!" (John 3:7 NKJV)*

EVANGELISM AND PASSOVER

Through salvation there is a connection between the Church and Passover. The Church spiritually participates in the Feast of Passover through the work of evangelists.

Passover was one of the three feasts that the Hebrews were commanded to keep each year. It is actually three feasts in one. The first day of the feast, Passover itself, was a celebration of the deliverance of the Hebrew children when the destroying angel "passed over" any home that had been marked on doorposts and lintel with the blood from a slain lamb.

The second part of Passover was the Feast of Unleavened Bread, a commemoration of the Hebrews' release and separation from bondage and slavery. The third part of the feast, First Fruits, memorialized their flight from Egypt, their march through the walls of water in the Red Sea, and their victorious arrival in the wilderness in freedom and new life.

While the New Testament Church is not commanded to physically or ritually keep the Feast of Passover, yet, since these feasts were to be kept forever (*Exodus 12:24*), the Church must keep them spiritually.

It is often the evangelist who leads the unsaved through the celebration of Passover. It is he who ties salvation or redemption to the shedding of blood and death by revealing that Jesus is the Passover Lamb (*1 Corinthians 5:7*). Through the shedding of His blood and His death on the cross people are saved, freed from the power of sin, and reconciled with the Father. In choosing to apply His blood to the doorposts of their hearts, they are cleansed and sanctified.

Then, an evangelist must tell the unsaved that Jesus is their unleavened bread. Since no trace of sin is found in Him, He is in fact the perfect but crushed Bread of Life (*John 6:35*). Finally, it is the evangelist who introduces new saints to Jesus, the First Fruit of the Father (*1 Corinthians 15:20*), the only One through whom they can gain new, powerful, resurrection life.

After His death on the cross Jesus was buried, remained in the grave for three days, and then rose from the dead. Similarly, each new saint goes through the same process in Him. Each dies to his old life of sin, each is buried, and each rises to new resurrection life in the kingdom of God and in right relationship with God the Father.

As Passover was not an optional celebration to the Hebrews, so salvation is not an optional event in the Church. It is a command! Any Church not actively engaged in evangelism, any Church which is not seeking to lead the unsaved through salvation and sanctification and into new, resurrection life does not know the will of God and is not keeping His feast. That Church is without life and power.

Today's fishers of men would do well to learn the fishing lesson taught to the early disciples by Jesus Himself. John 21 tells the story. After Christ's resurrection but before His ascension, several disciples had returned to the Sea of Galilee. They decided to go fishing. Accordingly, they jumped in a boat and spent all night toiling for fish. Although they labored long, the result was nothing. By themselves, they had caught not one fish.

When morning came, Jesus stood on shore. He commanded them to cast their net into the water. When they did so the catch was so huge they were not able to draw the fishing net into the boat (*John 21:6*). Then, upon recognizing Jesus, they dragged the net to shore and brought the fish to Him.

Some say that the Church has been in a long, dark night, that it has labored long in the flesh, that it has little or nothing to show for its efforts, and that for decades its numbers have been steadily decreasing. But a new day is dawning. The Lord is about to appear to His people once more. When He does so and issues His command for His catch, those empowered by His Holy Spirit will bring in a huge harvest of souls. With Jesus overseeing the operation, untold numbers of unsaved hearts will be caught in the net of His love and will be pulled out of the waters of darkness. Then these new saints will be brought to Jesus, their Savior, Lord, and King.

Today's fishers of men must fish in the way Jesus taught them. They must follow His ways in order to lead men to the Way. All should be emboldened by the truth of the words of the book of Romans that describe God's true evangelists:

> For "whoever calls upon the name of the LORD shall be saved." How then shall they call on Him in whom they have not believed? And how shall they believe in Him of whom they have not heard? And how shall they hear without a preacher? And how shall they preach unless they are sent? As it is written: "How beautiful are the feet of those who preach the gospel of peace, who bring glad tidings of good things!" Romans 10:13-15 (NKJV)

A COMPARISION

	THE GRACE	THE MINISTRY	THE EVANGELIST
REFERENCE:	• 2 Cor. 5:18 • 1 Peter 3:15 • Luke 24:47 • Acts 5:42	• 2 Cor. 5:18 • 1 Peter 3:15 • Luke 24:47 • Acts 5:42	• Ephesians 4:11 • 1 Peter 3:15 • John 6:44 • Galatians 1:6-12 • Acts 1:8 • Matthew 28:19-20
SOURCE:	Jesus	Jesus	• Father • Son • Holy Spirit
FROM WHOM:	the unsaved	the unsaved	the unsaved
WHEN:	always	always	always
PURPOSE:	bring the unsaved into the Kingdom of God	bring the unsaved into the Kingdom of God	bring the unsaved into the kingdom of God
METHODS:	presenting the good news that Jesus is *the* way by which people can be saved from sin and brought into right relationship with Father God	presenting the good news that Jesus is *the* way by which people can be saved from sin and brought into right relationship with Father God	presenting the good news that Jesus is *the* way by which people can be saved from sin and brought into right relationship with Father God

EVANGELISTS: THE FALSE

"....there are some who trouble you and want to pervert the gospel of Christ." Galatians 1:7 (NKJV)

While it is God's intention that an unbelieving people should hear the good news of Jesus Christ, it is the enemy's intention that they should not. While God wills that none should perish (2 *Timothy 3:9*) and that all people should spend eternity with Him in heaven, it is Satan's desire that all should perish and spend eternity with him in hell. As God raises up and sends out those who proclaim that salvation can only be found through the blood of Jesus Christ, so also, Satan raises up those and sends out those who are counterfeit ministers with a contrary message.

BAD CHARACTER

A FALSE EVANGELIST IS SELF-CENTERED: False evangelists do not have the character of true servants of God. False evangelists are not selfless; instead, they are self-centered.

The heart cry of a true evangelist is for the unsaved. The reality of unbelievers spending eternity in hell because they don't know Jesus sends this man of God out to the unsaved at all hours, in all conditions, and in all places to acquaint them with Jesus. He can rejoice only when the angels are rejoicing that another name has been added to the Book of Life.

A false evangelist, however, settles for far less. He's not concerned with the unsaved, but with himself. If no souls are saved at the end of his ministry in one town, he just complacently goes on to the next stop in his prearranged itinerary. He is more concerned with the size of his bank account and the coziness of his house than with saving souls. He seems unconcerned that in each community he enters and leaves, the unsaved remain unsaved and the saved are unchanged.

A FALSE EVANGELIST HAS A DISTORTED MIND: Carried to the extreme, false evangelists can be found among those who mark the last days, those who, if not disciplined and corrected, become

> ....*lovers of themselves, lovers of money, boasters, proud, blasphemers, disobedient to parents, unthankful, unholy, unloving, unforgiving, slanderers, without self-control, brutal, despisers of good, traitors, headstrong, haughty, and lovers of pleasure, rather than lovers of God. 2 Timothy 3:2-4 (NKJV)*

They hold a form of piety but are strangers to the power of it (2 *Timothy 3:5*). They are deceivers (2 *Timothy 3:6*), depraved, and reprobate (2 *Timothy 3:8*). They are hostile to the truth and use counterfeit means to distort the truth (2 Timothy 3:8). They worm their way into people's minds, hindering or preventing recognition or knowledge of the Truth, Jesus (2 Timothy 3:7). They not only don't represent God, they are anathema to Him.

WHAT DOES A FALSE EVANGELIST DO?

A true evangelist is one who proclaims the good news of forgiveness of sin and salvation from this world into the kingdom of God. A false evangelist is one who does not. His failures are apparent in several ways.

A FALSE EVANGELIST DISTRACTS FROM THE SPIRITU-AL: A false evangelist fails by his methods. If a true evangelist presents the good news, the false one either fails to do so or presents a different message detailing his erroneous version as to how an unbeliever can get to heaven. Since he knows or cares little about the spiritual aspect of new life, he is all too eager to draw the unsuspecting to himself through their minds or emotions. A false evangelist presents long-winded teachings or declares a way to new knowledge. He preys on fear, anger, and sorrow. In so doing he causes many would-be Christians to spend an exaggerated amount of time and effort dealing with the physical, mental, and emotional rather than the spiritual, with the external rather than the internal. By doing this, he halts their forward progress unto true salvation. This is presenting a contrary gospel message.

A FALSE EVANGELIST PREACHES A FALSE GOSPEL: As a false evangelist fails by his methods, so also he fails by his message. He speaks any word that leaves his hearers in their unsaved plight. He may preach a word that denies the need of salvation from sin. Another approach, if a false evangelist agrees that there is need for salvation, is to simply speak a false gospel message which declares that there is salvation in others besides Jesus or salvation in other ways (such as good works) than through the cleansing power of His shed blood. Or, in a deliberate attempt to confuse or divert, a false evangelist may place primary emphasis on man and how people, situations, and even deity relate to man rather than placing primary emphasis on God and showing how man relates to Him.

> **A false evangelist speaks a false word.**

The apostle Paul had described these false evangelists: *"... but there are some who trouble you and want to pervert the gospel of Christ" (Galatians 1:6-7 NKJV).*

And to these Paul has issued a solemn warning: *"But even if we, or an angel from heaven, preach any other gospel to you than what we have preached to you, let him be accursed" (Galatians 1:8 NKJV).*

This curse that becomes effective if the gospel is traumatized is repeated twice *(Galatians 1:9).* That repetition underscores its seriousness. Those purposefully presenting a false gospel and leading the lost to perdition are themselves doomed.

A FALSE EVANGELIST PRESENTS A FALSE GOD: Included in the nefarious message of the false evangelist is the bad news of other gods. A truly reprobate evangelist will preach about false gods (He may be one of them!) and lead the unsaved to them. Like the false apostle, a false evangelist does not build the Church of Jesus Christ; he tears it down. He doesn't add to the true Church but, in fact, he takes away from it. This disciple of Satan draws people away from the one true God and into the presence of his master, Satan.

A FALSE EVANGELIST COUNTERFEITS THE MIRACULOUS: Concerning the working of miracles, there is a contradiction in the Church. While it is supposed to be the unbelieving generation which seeks signs and wonders, today it is so often Christians who constantly and persistently seek the miraculous. If someone with a prophetic or healing ministry is announced as a guest speaker in a Church, the attendance at any given service is almost guaranteed to double. Christians today are so starved for the miraculous that they make spiritual giants out of anyone displaying the smallest grace of power. Worse, they often fail to discern the source of that power. One can only wonder to what degree this lust for power has led to fraud.

The signs and wonders are as false as he is.

Jesus sent the Holy Spirit to His Church to baptize His disciples with power so that they could be His witnesses to the very ends of the earth *(Acts 1:8)*. Unfortunately, false evangelists want His power for very different reasons. Rather than promote God, they want God and His power to promote themselves. In short, false evangelists want to use God; they want God and His power to aggrandize them and their ministries.

Signs, wonders, and miracles are very evident in the work of a true evangelist. God uses miracles to show people that He is God. He allows miracles to be a valid part of a true evangelist's ministry in order to draw people so that a gospel message can be presented with power. However, false evangelists just want the power. They covet it not to draw people to God, but to themselves. They lust after it to gain attention and to glorify themselves. This is the antithesis of what the Word instructs in *Acts 4:12 (NKJV): "Nor is there salvation in any other, for there is no other name under heaven given among men by which we must be saved."*

This "no other name" includes that of the false evangelist who wants to bring the glory of God down and confine it to his own tent. A false evangelist won't admit that his own name won't save and that signs and wonders can't save; only Jesus can.

The Word of God is very clear that miracles will not, in themselves, cause people to believe. In the Old Testament, in spite of witnessing many signs, Pharaoh did not believe *(Exodus 5-14).* In spite of repeated miracles, the Hebrews also did not believe *(Exodus 16:1-3).*

In the New Testament, this same lesson is learned in the story of a certain rich man *(Luke 16:19-31).* He had lived a life in luxury but was spending eternity in agony. In his efforts to get his family to hear and respond to the salvation message so that they would not share a similar fate, he lifted his voice and called out across the chasm to Abraham, asking him to send Lazarus, a saint enjoying the comforts of Paradise, to his father's house with a testimony of truth *(Luke 16:27)*. The rich man begged Abraham to allow Lazarus to miraculously return from the dead, go to his family, and evangelize them.

Abraham, giving more credence to the Word than to miracles, replied: *"They have Moses and the prophets; let them hear them" (Luke 16:29 NKJV).*

The rich man then denied the primary importance of the Word. He called out again, placing the emphasis of salvation on a sign or a miracle, hoping that this would save his family. He said, *"No, father Abraham; but if one goes to them from the dead, they will repent" (Luke 16:30 NKJV).*

This desire, this counterfeit, this false dependence on miracles rather than on the gospel to bring his unsaved family into a revelation of the Truth was utterly denied him. Again, putting primary importance on the good news rather than on signs or miracles, Abraham instructed the rich man and thereby all false evangelists: *"....If they do not hear Moses and the prophets, neither will they be persuaded though one rise from the dead" (Luke 16:31 NKJV).*

Jesus also knew that overemphasis could be placed on miracles and signs. He knew that some of the people around Him wanted bread (John 6:26), but they didn't want the Bread of Life (John 6:35). He knew that miracles could feed a need and lead to the gospel being preached, but He also knew that miracles may feed a greed and lead to a desire for gifts and power rather than the person or presence of Jesus.

LEVELS OF FALSE EVANGELISM

1. THE GRACE OF FALSE EVANGELISM: As with the other ascension gifts, there are three levels or areas of difficulty concerning false evangelists. The first is the mismanagement of the grace of evangelism. This may be a saint who is so fearful that he refuses to speak of the salvation of Jesus when opportunity presents. Or, it might be a saved one who has not learned Scripture well enough to understand his own salvation and so is unable to present it to others. He may try, but his efforts often end in confusion and failure.

2. THE MAN OF FLESH: Second, there is the man of flesh who operates under a human spirit. He is supposed to preach about the Lord and lead the unsaved to Jesus. In reality,

The man of flesh seeks fame and fortune.

he often preaches about himself and his own experiences and leads people to his own tent. Or, he may be a man whose primary motivation is financial rather than a burning desire to save the lost.

3. THE DISCIPLE OF SATAN: Third, there is the outright disciple of Satan who, operating under his evil spirit, preaches a false gospel and leads the unsaved to a false god or to the antichrist. While there is a difference in depravity, all three of these false evangelists are causing the Church great harm.

THE DOWNWARD SPIRAL

HE WANTS ATTENTION: The false evangelist, heady with power and the attention it brings him, may start out on a personal road to perdition by calling out a few false healings. Perhaps they will be false healings for headaches or backaches or other non-verifiable illnesses or infirmities. As chicanery grows, he'll magnify the healings, not the Healer.

HE NEEDS ATTENTION: Soon he'll progress from wanting attention to needing attention. As his sin and degradation continue in a downward spiral, he may even plant people in his audience who will claim false miracles of marriages saved, finances restored, or bodies healed. Justifying himself by claiming that these things are harmless or that they build faith, he promotes dishonesty, fraud, and fakery. He also claims that his deceptions build faith, ignoring the Word of God that *"... faith comes by hearing, and hearing by the Word of God"* (Romans 10:17 NKJV).

HE GROWS ADDICTED TO ATTENTION: When the need for power has led to an addiction to power, there is a further step of evil that lures the false evangelist. A truly apostate false evangelist will manifest miracles not by means of the Holy Spirit or even by fraudulent works of flesh. When truly given over to the enemy, a false evangelist will manifest miracles as a result of an unholy spirit.

Not content with introducing false gods, he'll manifest false miracles by the power of the gods he represents. For example, a false evangelist will display or promote healing practices such as hypnosis or psychic healing which spring from the deceptive and often occult power of false gods.

When the urge or demand for fame and power drive a false one to preach a false word or lead people to false gods, he isn't too particular where his power comes from. When he allows miracles to be done through him by an evil power guiding his thoughts, words, and deeds, he is a tool of the devil.

Like Jannes and Jambres, court magicians to Pharaoh, a false evangelist has a certain amount of power (*Exodus 7:11,22; 8:7*). However, there comes a time when that power ends (*Exodus 8:18*). There comes a time when it is evident to all that God's power goes far beyond magic in spite of anything man or Satan can do to deny it or copy it.

A false evangelist should also keep in mind that there comes a time when destruction overtakes false ministers: *"Now as Jannes and Jambres resisted Moses, so do these also resist the truth; men of corrupt minds, disapproved concerning the faith; but they will progress no further, for their folly will be manifest to all; as theirs also was"* (2 Timothy 3:8-9 NKJV).

WARNING: FALSE METHODS

Without the calling, the message or the nature of a true servant of the Lord, the false evangelist will fake or forgo true evangelism in his methods. This is discernible in several areas.

A FALSE EVANGELIST MAKES THE SHEEP DO HIS JOB: Since a true evangelist is one whose eagerness to reach the unsaved will take him out of the Church to where the unsaved are, a false evangelist is one who remains in the Church preaching to the saved. Whether because of ignorance, laziness, lack of authority, tradition, or because he's also acting as pastor and doesn't want to give up control of his Church and his captive flock, a false evangelist elects to remain with God's saved rather than to seek the unsaved.

Two immediate results of evangelizing in the wrong place are irresponsibility and accusation. For example, when a local Church invites an evangelist to come into an area, the false evangelist goes into their building, not into their community. He may precede his presence with an instruction to a pastor to be sure that the saints "Bring in the unsaved!" to hear his message. Some sheep do in fact try to excite friends or family to come to his services. Many though, from complacency or fear, fail to seek out the unsaved to invite them to meet Jesus.

The false evangelist then gets irritated with the pastor and lets him know that the crucially important message that God sent him to preach was wasted. The pastor, embarrassed at the apathy and poor showing, in turn gets angry at his flock and vents his displeasure. In such cases, the saints are both target and victim.

Does the fault of the failure lie with the sheep? Is it the sheep who have not done their job properly, or is it the false evangelist?

All may have a grace of evangelism, but do all have the gift? Should sheep be berated for not wholeheartedly doing something that man, not God, commanded them to do? Shouldn't the evangelist be out among the unsaved in order to lead them into the Church rather accusing the Church of failing the unsaved? Is he right to burden the saved with the responsibility to do his work for him?

Can't the evangelist understand that few unbelievers are comfortable in making life-changing decisions before a building full of strangers? Won't they realize that there would be a more eager response to the gospel message and certainly clearer understanding of it in a one-on-one visit by an evangelist in the homes of the unsaved—or where ever they may be found?

ROLE SWITCHING: A second faulty method used in counterfeit evangelism involves role switching. If all has gone ill and a false evangelist or a misguided pastor has not succeeded in hounding saints into bringing the lost into Church, a false evangelist, knowing his salvation message will fall on unhearing ears, will switch hats. He slides over his line of authority, blurs the limitations of his ministry, and functions in an area in which he may or may not hold office. Rather than preaching the gospel to the unsaved, he begins to preach or teach doctrine to the saved. He finds himself in

False evangelists don't do as God asked. They do as they please.

the wrong place speaking the wrong message to the wrong people. Rather than lose an audience, he bumbles on, but he doesn't do the job he was called to do.

A false evangelist will try to be all things to all people. He will not acknowledge that if a Church wants special ministry to *the unsaved* it should call for an evangelist. However, if it wants revival of or ministry to *its members,* it should send for preachers or teachers.

Another way that a false evangelist involves himself in role switching is by trying to keep the souls "he" saved.

A false evangelist tries to keep the souls "he" saved.

In this variation of error, rather than performing as a teacher, he tries to become a pastor. Instead of operating under the authority of a local Church, he sets himself up in opposition to it. Instead of leading baby lambs to the main flock, he decides to keep them and build his own flock. He mistakenly believes that since "he" saved them, they are his. The truth is that he didn't save them; God did. Therefore, they are not his, but His. As sheep of God's pasture, they belong in His flock.

A false evangelist fails to realize that the jobs of evangelism and pastoring are almost total opposites, and, as such, almost impossible for one man to do. For example, the evangelist works out of the Church; the pastor within. The evangelist brings them in; the pastor cares for them once they are in. The evangelist limits his preaching to the presentation of the salvation message; the pastor goes on from there, presenting the infinite riches and wonders of God.

It is virtually impossible for one man who is supposed to be out in the streets among the unsaved to spend the quality time needed in the Church to keep, tend, guide, and discipline the sheep. A better course of action for the evangelist would be to bring the sheep in, turn them over to the care of another who has been called by God as a shepherd, and then go back out for more.

There are some who have been gifted to serve in more than one office in the Church. However, others occupy multiple offices by their own choice, not God's. If an evangelist deviates from his true calling, if he changes hats and is consistently preaching, teaching, or overseeing rather than saving, either he is not an evangelist at all, or he has placed the lust for ministry above integrity.

WARNING: FALSE PRESENTATION

A FALSE EVANGELIST PREACHES ABOUT HIMSELF: In addition to problems with the operational methods of a false evangelist, there are also difficulties in what he expounds. A false evangelist, rather than preaching the gospel, will often preach himself. Rather than telling unbelievers that there is no other name than that of Jesus by which they can be saved (*Acts 4:12*), he will preach, glorify, and testify concerning his own name. In an orgy of ego, a false evangelist spotlights himself.

In the first days of ministry, a false evangelist may be careful to proclaim the good news of Jesus Christ, but as days pass, he will begin to intersperse the gospel with testimony of self rather than of the Lord. Soon, greater and greater proportions of his message deal with himself. Finally, Jesus is given only a cursory sentence or two out of the false evangelist's entire presentation while the personal experiences of the minister are aggrandized. When the words I, me, and my predominate, that ministry is false.

False evangelists don't know or don't care that a continuous recollection of their personal experiences will not lead people to Christ. Constantly quoting Revelations 12:11 and insinuating that this Scripture gives them the right to spend hours talking about themselves, they fail to realize that the primary importance of the verse is to detail a Christian's victory as it pertains to Christ in him. False evangelists refuse to admit that its primary emphasis should center on the testimony of Jesus, not of self. In pride and ego, they do not believe that it is the gospel, rather than personal testimony, which saves (Romans 1:16 NKJV).

False evangelists find it hard to admit that they are mere men, tempted and fallible. They, in putting their experiences on a par with the gospel of Christ, often fail to concede that they cannot offer the answer that He does. They fail to see that adding all the embellishments in the world to the gospel message will not offer mankind one thing of eternal value. Only the name and good news of Jesus will.

A FALSE EVANGELIST APPEALS THROUGH EMOTION: Another approach to problematic evangelism is by appeal to emotion. A false evangelist will appeal to the soul (mind, emotions, and personality of men) rather than to his heart or spirit. That makes his work one of flesh, not of Spirit. In his presentation of Jesus, this false evangelist will wring every drop of emotion out of the unsaved. He will appeal to every feeling known to mankind. Whether teasing, cajoling or frightening them, whether praising, flattering or condemning them, he works their flesh by his flesh. Again he forgets, or doesn't know, that the foundation of salvation is the gospel massage, not theatrics. The good news should be a message to man's spirit, not to his emotions.

A false evangelist appeals to intellect and emotion.

If this false minister wins any souls at all, they are converts of flesh. Nothing of eternal value has been presented to them so there are no eternal results. These are the ones who the true Church, in sorrow and in desperation for their souls, watches stray, backslide, and then revert to the ways of the world.

A FALSE EVANGELIST FAILS TO LAY A SOLID FOUNDATION: A third area of error in the presentation of the gospel involves failing to lay the proper foundation of faith: Jesus. While a true evangelist will build a foundation on who Jesus is and what He has already done at the cross, a false evangelist will concentrate on who the unsaved are and what Jesus could or ought to do concerning their needs. To lure them, he makes all kinds of false promises to them. In other words, by concentrating on the sinner and not on the Savior, he lays a faulty, weak, wrong foundation for faith.

Those things that a false evangelist places lowest on the list of things he considers important for salvation— **A false evangelist lays a weak, faulty foundation.** like bringing a lost one to acknowledge his sin, repenting, confessing sin, surrendering unconditionally, receiving forgiveness, and reconciling with God—are of highest priority to God. Conversely, those things that man seems to place highest—like ensuring that his own needs and desires will be met before he will commit himself to Christ—God places lowest.

A false evangelist then actively perverts the salvation process by reversing God's order. He introduces salvation as a way to meet people's requirements, not God's. He doesn't understand that his erroneous methods teach people to sell themselves to whomever they think is the highest bidder. A false evangelist bases salvation on people's demand to fill their needs as declared by themselves rather than on their real need which is reconciliation with the Father as declared by Jesus Christ: *"You must be born again"* [emphasis added] *(John 3:7 NKJV).*

False evangelists do not see the similarity between marriage and salvation. They don't know that, humanly speaking, all too many women marry for the wrong reasons. These women may marry to escape a bad home life, to obtain money and material goods, to gain social prestige, or to take what they can get because they believe they may never get a better offer. These faulty foundations will produce a shaky marriage. If marriage was not enjoined for right reasons, it will not be an honorable estate. And, since its base is weak, if it is pushed too hard or pressured too much, it may collapse.

Just so, too many saints have entered marriage to the Lamb for wrong reasons. Many have come into God's kingdom as a result of a false evangelist building a false foundation in their marriage to Jesus. A false evangelist will attract and seek to marry unbelievers to Jesus for wrong reasons. He may portray Jesus as the only way to escape hell, as the Provider of all material goods, or as the One who can help the unsaved climb not the social but the sacred ladder (perhaps with the lure of ministry). Or, he may convince believers that they probably can't do any better so they might as will take Jesus.

While all of these needs can be fulfilled in Jesus, they should not be laid as the cornerstones of salvation. Healing heals, but it doesn't save. Provision provides, but it doesn't save. Jesus the sacrificial Lamb is the only proper foundation for salvation, not Jesus the Healer or Jesus the Provider.

True salvation is based on the unbeliever's recognition of his sin, his separation from the Father, and his acknowledgement of his need of reconciliation with the Father. True salvation is rightly founded on what Jesus has done for mankind by going to the cross and shedding His blood for the forgiveness of the sins and on what the sinner's response to that act of love is by asking Him to be his personal Savior. True salvation is not based on the rather vague promises of a false evangelist about what Jesus might do for the sinner once he is saved or on the sinner's own demands on Jesus.

To those who neither know nor respect God yet who try to represent Him, Jesus is sometimes portrayed as a holy Santa Claus with an endless bag of goodies with which He will unquestionably fill all needs. Rather than Savior, Jesus is emphasized as Healer, Provider, Comforter, Leader, or Peace-giver. Surely, He is all these, but false evangelists neglect to mention that, except by a sovereign act of a loving God, right relationship to God precedes and takes precedence over these other aspects. While these other aspects are building blocks of the faith, they are blocks built on the foundation of Jesus' atoning work on the cross.

As in the earthly marriage relationship, these imperfect foundations can't hold weight. When the evangelized discover that God cannot and will not be manipulated, that He will not pour forth gifts on demand as has been implied, that He desires faithfulness rather than harlotry and obedience rather than greed, the blush of romance quickly cools. As the foundation crumbles, the misled, angry at God, fall away.

A FALSE EVANGELIST IS A SHOWMAN: Yet another way that a false evangelist errors in his presentation of the gospel involves showmanship. Heedless of the teaching of Paul who stated that preaching is to be without eloquence lest the cross of Christ should be deprived of force, emptied of power, and made void of value(1 Corinthians 1:17), a false evangelist promotes the presentation, not the gospel message.

Some false evangelists pretend to reach the unsaved with an elaborate, well-rehearsed speech that includes perfectly timed gestures, expressions of emotion, intonations, and special effects. Sweat pores off his forehead, and spittle flies out of his mouth. The only person affected by all this is the false evangelist himself. The unsaved just sit there and watch the show.

Other false evangelists use a choir, band, or other music ministry as their gospel message. They think that just

A false evangelist is a showman, not a servant of God.

one tune sung or played loudly or long enough will bring hoards of the hurting into the kingdom. There is no question music can aid in the presentation of the gospel message, but even if so presented, it is the good news itself, not rhythm, melody, beat, clarity of voices, or sounds of instruments that will save souls. If a musical presentation glorifies flesh, human talents or abilities, instruments, or sound systems, that is a false ministry. If a minister glorifies the presentation of the message of salvation rather than the content of the true gospel of God, that man is a false evangelist.

THE FRUIT OF A FALSE EVANGELIST

The result of the work of a false evangelist is spurious. It resembles the truth in appearance but not in fact. It is impossible to estimate the damage it has done to the true church of God.

THE DEAD DON'T LIVE: One fruit of the work of a false evangelist is that the dead stay dead. Those who have not heard the good news don't get to hear it from him. If an evangelist will not go where the unsaved are, the unsaved stay unsaved. There are very few salvations and even fewer baptisms evidenced in his work.

THE LIVING DIE: A second consequence of the work of a false evangelist is that the living suffer. True salvation is the basis of an eternal walk with God. Once saved, saints are not to keep laying the same foundation. Once saved, they are to build on the living foundation, Jesus. Repeating ad infinitum the glories of the salvation message is not going to save those already saved; nor is it going to feed them. It is not going to mature them. When a false evangelist keeps a local Church forever at step one, all growth and life stop. The Church dies.

BACKSLIDING: A third result is backsliding. A false evangelist's work is characterized by the temporal, not the eternal. The results of egging someone into the kingdom as a result of personal experience, emotional appeal, showmanship, or questionable miracles cannot last. If there is no foundation on the Rock, the shelter of salvation will fall. Those who slid into the Church through false expectation, false miracles, false promises, false gospels, or false gods eventually slide right back out again.

If Jesus is not both the author and foundation of salvation there is no salvation. There may be temporary interest, but if salvation is centered on anything other than Christ, that interest won't last. It will not carry anyone through difficult times.

DISILLUSIONMENT: A fourth result of all this nefarious activity is disillusionment. The ultimate evil of false evangelism is that people get disappointed not with the false evangelist, but with the true God who was so falsely and deceptively represented.

Evangelism is the introduction of the lost to the Lord and then to His body, the Church. If that acquaintanceship goes awry, so may the unsaved. When a false evangelist is offensive in his message and his methods, he may actually keep away, send away, or turn off the very souls he tried to save. He may so brutalize, deceive, and disillusion the lost that they may never find the Lord.

As a false fisherman of souls, he will ultimately stand before God for an accounting of his ministry. True to form, he will probably spend most of his time lying to God about the ones who got away.

OUR RESPONSE TO THE FALSE EVANGELIST

As with the previous studies of the ministries of false apostles and counterfeit prophets, shining the light of truth on the lie of false evangelism has exposed it for the danger that it is. Steps must be taken to correct error and then to guard against it.

TEST THE SPIRITS: First and foremost, to protect themselves and the Church from the deceptive ministrations of a false evangelist, all saints must learn to discern. As the Word commands, all saints are to test the spirits (1 John 4:1).

Concerning a false evangelist, saints must discern in their spirit whether he is one sent by God to seek the lost, one sent by self to seek attention and power, or one sent by the enemy to seek destruction. More specifically, has he come in God's name or that of another? Has he come in God's power or that of another? A crucial question for each saint to ponder is whether or not we or our Church have received or given approval to the work of enemy agents of evangelism. Have we been like those described by John?

> I have come in My Father's name and with His power and you do not receive me—your hearts are not open to Me, you give Me no welcome. But if another comes in his own name and his own power and with no other authority but himself, you will receive him and give him your approval. John 5:43 (TAB)

REPENT: Second, the Church must repent. If the body of Christ has allowed false evangelism to exist as a false ministry in our midst or tolerated it without correcting it, we must confess our sin and then ask for and receive forgiveness for it. Then we must totally turn from that evil which places both the saved and the unsaved under bondage.

REVIEW AND RENEW THE FOUNDATION OF OUR SALVATION: Further, we must review our own salvation. Was it the product of desire for reconciliation with the Father through the Son, or for another reason? Was our salvation the result of a dependence on the evangelist or of emotional stress? Was it the fruit of the gospel being attractively but shallowly presented? Was our salvation based on false doctrine, false gospel, false gods, or denominationalism? Did a hope of healing or a promise of provision take precedence over the presence of Jesus in our heart? In short, although married to Him, are we married for the wrong reasons, and is our union with Him shaky?

If so, we must humble ourselves before the Lord. We must set right the base of our salvation, the foundation of our faith. We must approach our Husband, confess our sin and repent before Him. We must ask Him to forgive us for trying to make Him meet our demands and stipulations for salvation rather than making us meet His. We must receive the forgiveness granted to us, and then renew our marriage vows to Jesus, this time for the right reason.

DEAL WITH THE BAD NEWS: When our relationship with the Lord is on a solid foundation, we must go on. In making right the wrongs of false evangelism we must understand that God is eager to expose lies.

We must understand that a false evangelist spreads bad news, not God's good news. The people of God must refute such evil tidings with truth, not lies, and reality, not desire. We must test the spirits in order to discern the source of the bad news and then apply biblical principles in our warfare against it.

The Church must also deal with the preaching of another gospel. Rather than denying that problems exist in evangelism, the Church must face the situation and get on with the correction and discipline of its members. False evangelism can only be dealt with once it is recognized and understood as the huge problem that it is.

Also, individually and as a Church, we must reject all ministries of evil. God's Word is very clear on this. False ministers, those who would send people to hell rather than to save them, must be confronted and dealt with.

Following the godly principles of correction and, if need be, discipline found in Matthew 18:15-17, false ministers must be held accountable to the Church. If at any point in the disciplinary process, they repent of their evil ways, God is well served. If they will not, Scripture has clear instructions to the saints:

> Avoid [all] such people--turn away from them.
> 2 Timothy 3:5 (TAB)

> They have depraved and distorted minds, and are reprobate and counterfeit and to be rejected as far as the faith is concerned. 2 Timothy 3:8 (TAB)

REBUILD THE FOUNDATION: Another thing that we must do to correct evangelistic abuse is to get back to basics. Fakery and chicanery have poisoned some minds and led many astray. Yet those who are lost need to know the truth now more than ever. The need for true evangelism and truth in evangelism has never been more prevalent than it is now.

The Church needs to return to the Word, learn it, and preach it as a foundation for correcting error. Also, from the Word, the Church should properly train those raised up by God as evangelists and then send them out as an army that desires to lead the unsaved to Jesus. Further, we should know that God has raised every saint in the Church to be His ministers of reconciliation (2 *Corinthians* 5:18). Along with those who are true evangelists in the universal Church, every saint must accept the grace of evangelism and go forth.

The good news is not good news to those who have never heard it. We must go house to house (*Acts* 5:42). We must go nation to nation (*Matthew* 28:19-20). We must assure the unsaved of a warm welcome in the arms of Jesus (*John* 6:37).

Some who may have been thwarted or disillusioned by a false evangelist now claim that Christianity is an exclusive religion. Nothing could be farther from the truth. In fact, it is the most inclusive. God is unwilling that any should perish but desires that all come to repentance (2 *Peter* 3:9). He sent His Son that whosoever should call on the name of the Lord would not perish but have eternal life with Him (*John* 3:16).

Aided by the Father who draws all men unto Jesus (*John* 6:44), by Jesus who calls out to the unsaved and who is the revealer of the gospel (*Galatians* 1:6,12), and by the power of the Holy Spirit (Acts 1:8), we must become like those of an earlier day who turned the world upside down as they proclaimed the death and resurrection of Christ—the gospel of Jesus (Acts 17:6).

EVANGELISTS

	THE TRUE	THE FALSE
CHARACTER:	• God centered • clear minded	• self or Satan centered • distorted minded
PURPOSE:	preach the good news of salvation through the blood of Jesus	fail or refuse to preach the good news but entice with a contrary word
LEVELS:	**THE GRACE:** the inexperienced who are occasionally used by God to share the good news **THE MINISTER:** those who present the good news in the local Church and community with increasing numbers being saved and led into the local Church **THE EVANGELIST:** those who present the good news throughout the world and whose ministry is often accompanied by signs and wonders	• the inexperienced who refuse to share the good news or who minister from a base of ignorance or fear • the men of flesh whose primary interest is acquisition of fame and fortune • the agents of Satan who present a false message of salvation through any means other than faith in the shed blood of Jesus Christ and whose "ministry" is rife with false miracles

| METHODS: | • they are out of the Church building ministering
• their weapon is the Word of God
• signs and wonders from the Spirit of God
• they lead the saved into Church | • they are everywhere, even in church to lure the unwary
• their weapon is contrary word
• signs and wonders from a different spirit
• they lead the unwary out of Church |

PASTORS: THE TRUE

"And He Himself gave some to be... pastors...."
Ephesians 4:11 (NKJV)

Going on in our study, the fourth ascension gift given by Jesus to some in the Church is the pastor *(Ephesians 4:11)*. It has often been wisely stated that while evangelists catch the fish, the pastors clean them.

Within the body of Christ there is rampant confusion concerning the function of pastors. Some of the problem comes from the lack of understanding as to the full extent or entire scope of this ministry. This lack of comprehension stems, at least in part, from the limitations of the English language in properly expressing or wholly translating the full meaning of Greek words.

In his book, *Restoring God's Church*, the late Derek Prince addresses this issue concerning pastors. From him we learn that there are several words in the Greek language—elder, shepherd, bishop, and overseer—which all refer to what the English language translates as but one word: pastor.

In other words, the titles of elder, shepherd, bishop, overseer, and pastor all refer to one person. Though misunderstood and therefore at times mislabeled by various denominations, these are not separate positions, titles, or ministries. Biblically speaking, they are simply different names for different aspects of the same ascension gift of pastor. While all these names or titles refer to one person or one job, the different words delineate and describe the many functions of the pastoral ministry.

A pastor is a shepherd, a bishop, an overseer, and an elder.

For instance, the words bishop and overseer can be used interchangeably, and they describe an elder's work in watching over or looking after the flock. The words shepherd and pastor are similar, and they portray the elder's work of tending to or caring for the sheep.

The statement that all these descriptive words refer to only one ascension gift may be difficult to accept. Therefore, it is essential to prove its veracity. That a pastor is a shepherd, a bishop, an elder, and an overseer can be ascertained by a careful look at Scripture.

PASTORS AND SHEPHERDS: First, a quick study in *The New Strong's Exhaustive Concordance of the Bible* shows that the Greek words for pastors and shepherds are the same. *Ephesians 4:11 (NKJV) says, "And He gave some to be....pastors."* The Greek word for pastors is *poimen*. Interestingly, this seems to be the only place in the New Testament where the word *poimen* is translated by the English word pastor. However, this same Greek word, *poimen*, is frequently translated as the English word shepherd. Consider the well-known verse *Luke 2:8 (NKJV)*: *"Now there were in the same country shepherds living out in the fields keeping watch over their flock by night."* Since the word *poimen*, or pastor, used in Ephesians 4:11 is the same as that used here to describe a shepherd, a *poimen* is both a pastor and a shepherd[1]. Therefore, pastors and shepherds are one.

BISHOPS AND OVERSEERS: Next, it can be ascertained that bishops and overseers are similar functions. First, concerning bishops, 1 Peter 2:25 declares that the Lord is a Bishop. *"For you were going astray like [so many] but now you have come back to the Shepherd and Guardian (the Bishop) of your souls"* (1 Peter 2:25 TAB). The Greek word used for guardian or bishop is *episkopos*.

Then concerning overseers, *Acts 20:28 (NKJV) says*: *"Therefore take heed to yourselves and to all the flock, among which the Holy Spirit has made you overseers...."* The Greek word used for the word overseers is also *episkopos*[2]. Therefore, bishops and overseers are one and the same.

ELDERS: There is another function of the ascension gift of pastor to consider. That is the ministry of the elder. According to *Vine's Expository Dictionary of Biblical Words*, the <u>word elder is f</u>rom the Greek word *presbuteros*[3]. It refers

---

1. *Both pastor and shepherd have The New Strong's Exhaustive Concordance of the Bible number 4165, poimano, "to tend as a shepherd, supervise, rule."*
2. *Both bishop and overseer have The New Strong's Exhaustive Concordance of the Bible number 1983, episkopeo, "to oversee, take oversight."*
3. *Co-elder has The New Strong's Exhaustive Concordance of the Bible number 4859, sumpresbtteros, "an elder or co-presbyter."*

to those who are older by age or those who are senior in rank or position of responsibility. Having met the qualifications for elder as listed in 1 Timothy 3 and Titus 1, they are charged with the spiritual care and oversight of the New Testament Church.

Having understood all this, it is necessary to see if there is a relationship with a bishop-overseer, a shepherd-pastor, and an elder. Peter gives us the answer in his first epistle:

> The **elders**[4] who are among you I exhort, I who am a fellow elder and a witness of the sufferings of Christ, and also a partaker of the glory that will be revealed: **Shepherd** the flock of God which is among you, serving as overseers, not by constraint but willingly, not for dishonest gain but eagerly. [emphasis added] 1 Peter 5:1-2 (NKJV)

In 1 Peter 5:1, it is the elders who are being addressed. Specifically, according to verse 2, they are being urged to shepherd (care for, tend, pastor) the flock of God and to do so in the capacity of an overseer or bishop. In other words, it is elders who were commissioned to shepherd, pastor, bishop, and oversee the new Church.

Thus, elder, bishop, overseer, and pastor are the same. It is one office that has several closely related functions. Since we can now more fully comprehend that a reference to any one of these words is alluding to but one ascension gift, we must now learn more about the work of that office.

---

4. Co-elder has *The New Strong's Exhaustive Concordance of the Bible* number 4859, *sumpresbuteros*, *"an elder or co-presbyter."*

GOOD CHARACTER

HEART OF LOVE: A shepherd's most obvious characteristic and certainly the greatest mark of a true pastor of God is a heart of love. God would not assign anyone to represent Him as a pastor who would not lovingly care for His sheep. He would not raise anyone to be a shepherd who could not express His own heart of love to His sheep.

As any mother can testify, those who are successful in caretaking roles must be motivated by love. Without love, there is no true care or caring. Without love, there is no true nursing, guiding, or watching over. Without love, there is nothing but duty.

Admittedly, all that a pastor's job entails can be mechanically done or performed without love. But that is exactly what it is—an act or a performance. Unloving works are works of flesh, fruitful for nothing. Any true shepherd must acknowledge that love is a primary prerequisite for a life of caring.

A shepherd loves his sheep.

DILIGENCE: A second characteristic of a pastor is diligence. He is always on the alert and constantly watching over the flock. He never goes off-duty. He provides constant attention to his charges and is meticulous in his care of them. He dares not slack off on his job for any reason because he knows that he is accountable concerning the sheep, for better or for worse, to another Shepherd.

WHAT DOES A PASTOR DO?

A shepherd must learn all that he can about his gift. His best source of information about his calling is his Bible. Throughout much of Scripture, the pastor is alluded to. Ezekiel 34:11-15 describes the merciful ministrations of a faithful shepherd. Much of his job description is echoed in the New Testament in the book of John, chapter ten. If one called by God to lead His flock can understand the correct functioning of the shepherds who care for sheep, he can better understand his own calling as a shepherd who cares for people. A comparison of the two is most helpful.

A SHEPHERD KNOWS HIS CALLING: First, before a person can function as a shepherd, he must be sure of his calling. He must be called or asked to be a shepherd by the one who owns the sheep. A man doesn't just become a shepherd for no good reason. He must have a desire to be a shepherd and have the right character and quali-ties. If there is no true call to pastoring in his heart, he is a shepherd for the wrong reasons and will do a poor job.

Just so, in God's kingdom shepherds are given their office by Jesus. It is the Lord who raises up spiritual shep-herds or overseers of the spiritual flock *(2 Samuel 5:2).* This is His privilege because the sheep are His. God calls some, but not all, ministers to serve as pastors. Thus, if the call to serve was not whispered within and confirmed without by the Lord Himself, then that is not a true, godly call to the office of pastor. If the call came from self, man, or denomination, it is but a work of flesh.

A TRUE SHEPHERD ACTS FOR THE OWNER OF THE SHEEP: A worldly shepherd works for his employer, the owner of the sheep. He is the owner's representative of

The sheep belong to God. the sheep and exercises the owner's government over them by ruling them with a just hand. So too, God's pastor knows that the sheep in his care are not his; they are His. He does not take lightly the knowledge that he is directly accountable to God for them. He knows that he is God's representative and is charged to exercise God's government over them.

A TRUE SHEPHERD CARES FOR THOSE ASSIGNED TO HIM: Next, a worldly shepherd is one who will search for and seek out the flock assigned to him. He is charged to care for his master's sheep, not for those of others. Specifically, he must spend time searching out and finding the sheep he is meant to tend.

Similarly, God's true shepherd does not shepherd just any old sheep. He knows that his sheep belong to God and that he has been assigned the caretaking duties of but a small portion of His whole flock. God's shepherd is not authorized to care for anyone else's sheep, but he must search out, find, and maintain leadership over those apportioned to him (*Ezekiel 34:11*). He is neither to ignore or reject sheep from his assigned flock nor to entice or outright steal sheep from another flock to add to his own. He simply oversees those God meant for him to pastor.

A TRUE SHEPHERD IS FOUND AMONG HIS SHEEP: Third, a worldly shepherd will always be found among

A true shepherd is found in the midst of his flock. his sheep. He is always present with his flock because he knows how quickly the need for him can arise. He knows that injuries, sickness, or changing weather conditions must be dealt with quickly, and they cannot be dealt with quickly if

he is on the next hill or in a different, distant pasture.

In like manner, God's shepherd must stay with the sheep *(Ezekiel 34:12)*. Those with the grace or ministry of pastoring find that their main ministry is to the local Church. He must care for his sheep and administrate godly government on a continuous rather than a sporadic basis, and that means being ever present among the ones over which he governs. He is married to his flock and is not meant to be an absentee husband. He should be with his family, not constantly out on the road.

A TRUE SHEPHERD KNOWS HIS SHEEP: In the manner of Jesus, God's true shepherd knows his sheep. He knows which of them are leaders and which are followers. He knows their strengths and weaknesses. He knows their histories or their shared stories of joy and sorrow.

God's true shepherd calls his sheep by name. He sees each as a person, not as a number. He is intimately aware of each as a member of his flock and cares for each individually, not just corporately.

A TRUE SHEPHERD SEEKS THE LOST: A worldly shepherd, knowing his accountability to the owner of the flock, will go out and look for lost and scattered sheep. He will not allow them to stay lost or alone for he knows if they do so they are easy targets for predators.

Just so, the true shepherd of God delivers his sheep from the places they have been scattered (*Ezekiel 23:12*). He seeks out and rescues the lost. He brings them back into the unity and strength of the flock and does his utmost to keep the flock intact. The shepherd knows there are wolves that like to feed on lambs and sheep. He knows a sheep separated from the flock is vulnerable. He knows that lone sheep, whether hurting, lost, or rebellious, are prey for wolves that delight to gobble them up. A true shepherd simply won't allow that to happen. Rather than lose a sheep, he will rescue it; he will deliver it from evil.

A TRUE SHEPHERD PROTECTS HIS FLOCK: In addition to seeking lone or lost sheep, a worldly shepherd will protect his flock. He will not allow thieves, robbers, or destroyers among his sheep.

God's shepherd is commanded to protect His sheep from wolves within and without too. He cannot allow anyone over the wall of the sheepfold (*John 10:1*). He cannot allow thieves and robbers to infiltrate or destroyers to scatter. When he sees a wolf coming, he will stand fast, protect his sheep, and not allow them to be scattered or destroyed. If necessary, he will lay down his life to save theirs (*John 10:11*).

A TRUE SHEPHERD TENDS HIS FLOCK IN AN AS-SIGNED SPACE: A worldly shepherd brings his sheep to their own land. He has often grown up in a pastoral setting. He knows from personal experience the hills, lakes, and streams; best feeding spots; and places of shelter. His pastoral heart will lead his sheep to the very best of these.

In the same manner, God's shepherd knows spiritual hills and valleys, watering spots, and deserts. He knows the limits and boundaries of his land. He brings his sheep into their own land, into the fullness of the area they were meant to occupy. However, he is careful not to let them go too far. He brings them to a place they can call their own but takes care not to encroach or outright poach on another's land. He will stay within his godly appointed limits of ministry and keep his sheep within their proper boundaries too.

A TRUE SHEPHERD LEADS: A worldly shepherd leads, not drives, his sheep. With crook in hand, he will go before the flock and lead them rather than stand behind them and drive them with a stick.

Similarly, God's shepherd will lead rather than drive His sheep (*John 10:3-4*). This shepherd enjoys the confidence of His sheep. If he leads, they will follow. Oftentimes, because of fear, sheep will not willingly go into what they perceive as a new or threatening situation. However, if led by a good, godly shepherd, they easily and willfully follow him into new pastures and new experiences.

A TRUE SHEPHERD FEEDS: A worldly shepherd will feed his flock. He will lead them to good pasture and see that they are filled.

A true shepherd of God will also see his flock fed (*Ezekiel 23:13; John 10:9*). He will lead them to good, rich pasture, not to bad. He is aware that some feeding places are fat, lush grounds that provide good feeding and that some are bad areas containing poisonous weeds. A true pastor will never allow his sheep to feed on the poison of the world. Instead he will lead them to the nourishment of the Word. He'll see that they feed on the Word, are filled by the Word, chew the Word, and digest the Word. He'll lead them to the fattest or best pastures of Scriptures and to the highest mountains of chapter and verse.

A TRUE SHEPHERD QUENCHES THIRST: A shepherd of the world must lead his sheep to water. In barren land, there are many dry places. A good shepherd must know where to find water. He also must test the water to be sure it is sweet and good before allowing the sheep to be refreshed by it.

Similarly, a true pastor will lead his flock to the deep pools and the flowing waters of the living God (*Ezekiel 23:14*). He allows them to quench their thirst in the streams of rejoicing. He'll see that they drink deeply so that the inner sheep is renewed and refreshed.

A TRUE SHEPHERD LEADS HIS SHEEP TO REST: A worldly shepherd will lead his flock to rest. In order to maintain strength and to remain healthy, he knows there are days and seasons when they must rest.

God's pastor also knows that he must lead the flock into rest *(Ezekiel 23:15)*. He knows there are times when exertion must cease. At such times he will lead his charges into a good fold or a shady, lush meadow and cause them to lie down. Knowing that fleshly effort is not of God, he will lead them into spiritual rest.

A TRUE SHEPHERD HEALS: A shepherd of the world is in charge of his flock's health. It is he who must bind wounds, attend to broken bones, give medicine, and pay close attention to his sheep's special needs during the time of recovery. If parasites and bugs begin to bother his sheep, he gets rid of them.

Applying godly principles to the health needs of the flock, God's shepherds will bind up that which was broken and strengthen that which was sick *(Ezekiel 34:16)*. They will treat all hurts and woes with tender care. They will cover all brokenness with love. They prayerfully anoint the sick with oil *(James 5:14)*. God's shepherds wrap all injuries and treat all disease with generous doses of the Holy Spirit. They lovingly and mercifully nurse their broken and sick ones back to health. If necessary, they know how and when to aid in deliverance from spiritual parasites or vermin, the demonic forces which plague and oppress the sheep.

A TRUE SHEPERD GIVES LIFE TO HIS SHEEP: A shepherd of the world brings life to his sheep. He not only keeps them well or nurses them to health, but he imparts life to them.

So, too, a true shepherd of God brings life to his flock (*John 10:10*). With Jesus as his pattern, he brings life not just to the body of a sheep; he watches over its soul and spirit as well. He is concerned for the inner being of his flock as well as the outer, and he tends and nourishes and nurtures it carefully. He is able, in the process of giving life to others, to reveal the Source of all life, Jesus Christ.

A TRUE SHEPHERD TEACHES: Having seen the monumental task of caretaking that is assigned to an elder, we must also consider that he is called to teach (*1 Timothy 3:2*). When an evangelist has done his job, has led the unsaved to the Lord and turned them over to the care of a godly pastor, those new saints are in need of teaching as well as of care. Worldly ways are not God's ways. Having spent their whole life until the moment of their salvation in the world and steeped in its sin, it is without question that new sheep need to be taught about God, His Word, His will, and His ways.

The Bible states that to the unsaved, the ways of God are foolishness (*1 Corinthians 2:14*). The unsaved do not understand the Word (or the Word made flesh) and cannot comprehend Jesus and His ways. Many think they do; many may try to; but the understanding of God's Word is impossible to those who are perishing in the world. The kingdom of God can be revealed only when the unsaved have acknowledged Jesus as Savior.

When this happens, when a sinner becomes a saint, the new lamb has the veil taken from her eyes. The kingdom of God then becomes real to her. She knows her eternal life is in the eternal Son. She realizes that she is a part of a new world or of a new kingdom and that she must learn about this new life in order to be able to walk in it successfully. After being brought into the fold by the rebirthing process during which she calls Jesus her Savior, she must also be taught that Jesus is Lord.

Further, it is not only baby lambs that need training. Sheep of every age never outgrow the need to learn. Once launched into the flock, they still need to grow and mature.

This teaching or preaching or imparting knowledge about kingdom life and the Source of that life, Jesus, is a job of the pastor. The pastor must not only shepherd and oversee his sheep, but he also must guide them through their life changes. He must teach them the rules of the kingdom, its judgments and statues (*Ezekiel 37:24*). He must teach and preach the Word for doctrine and for instruction in righteousness (*2 Timothy 3:16*). He must use it to set the standard of behavior for life in God's kingdom.

A TRUE SHEPERD DISCIPLINES: At times a rebellious sheep will wander astray. Worse, he will try to lead other sheep away too. For his own protection and that of the whole flock, there are times when he must be disciplined

In the Church, if God's standards are ignored or rebelled against, His shepherd must use the Word for reproof and correction (*2 Timothy 3:16*). Having taught the Word, if it is then violated, a pastor must discipline.

The civil governments of the world make it clear that they will not tolerate violation of their laws. They have established rules to deal with disorder and lawlessness and to bring offenders into a court of law for trial and possibly for punishment.

In the kingdom of God, when godly standards are rebelled against, the offenders are even more accountable. In this case, the offense is much more serious since it is not man and civil government that has been sinned against, but God and His government. Since a pastor is God's governor or ruler *(Matthew 2:6)*, he is charged with vindicating God's rules by actively instituting a disciplinary process among the rebellious.

Thus, a shepherd cares for, teaches, and disciplines the flock of God. In the local Church, his responsibilities cover all the needs of the sheep. As a caretaker, he visits, nurses, tends, watches over, looks after, and protects. As a teacher, he guides, leads, nourishes, and feeds. As a disciplinarian, he seeks out, corrects, and restores. The scope of this very important office us summed up in the Lord's own command to Peter concerning the new Church:

> *"Feed my lambs." (John 21:15)*

> *"Tend My sheep." (John 21:16)*

> *"Feed My sheep." (John 21:17)*

GOD'S SHEPHERDS

God's pastors can be compared to shepherds. There is one big difference, though. While earthly pastors are worldly keepers of physical animals, godly shepherds are spiritual leaders who care for a spiritual flock. God's pastors are the shepherds and guardians of the souls of God's sheep, the saints *(1 Peter 2:25)*. Their basic job is to guard, guide, and govern God's flock.

LEVELS OF PASTORING

1. THE GRACE: The first level are the men or women who lead or have oversight over a home group or local Church. If they do God's will in caring for God's sheep, they may be asked to assume more responsibility.

2. THE MINISTRY: One with the ministry of pastoring may find himself overseeing several Churches or an area wide grouping of them.

3. THE OFFICE OF PASTOR: The one with the ascension gift of pastor has a reach far greater and an influence far deeper. Because of his care for God's family, his ability to govern well, and the excellence of his character, he may find himself a caretaker in the universal Church, a pastor of pastors.

HOW IS A PASTOR CHOSEN?

A saint does not become a pastor by deciding to be one or by declaring himself to be one. Nor does he become one simply upon the basis of graduation from Bible school. A saint becomes a pastor in obedience to the call of God on his life. He is raised by God and given his position by Jesus.

QUALIFICATIONS FOR OFFICE

Any pastor must meet stringent requirements before he can be loosed for service. Since a pastor is an elder, he must meet God's qualifications earlier referred to in Scripture:

> *This is a faithful saying: If a man desires the position of a bishop, he desires a good work. A bishop then must be blameless, the husband of one wife, temperate, sober-minded, of good behavior, hospitable, able to teach; not given to wine, not violent, not greedy for money, but gentle, not quarrelsome, not covetous; one who rules his own house well, having his children in submission with all reverence (for if a man does not know how to rule his own house, how will he take care of the church of God?); not a novice, lest being puffed up with pride he fall into the same condemnation as the devil. Moreover he must have a good testimony among those who are outside, lest he fall into reproach and the snare of the devil. 1 Timothy 3:1-7 (NKJV)*

Also concerning elders (bishops, overseers, shepherds, pastors) are the words of Titus:

> *....appoint elders in every city as I commanded you—if a man is blameless, the husband of one wife, having faithful children not accused of dissipation or insubordination. For a bishop must be blameless, as a steward of God, not self-willed, not quick-tempered, not given to wine, not violent, not greedy for*

money, but hospitable, a lover of what is good, sober-minded, just, holy, self-controlled, holding fast the faithful word as he has been taught, that he may be able, by sound doctrine, both to exhort and convict those who contradict. Titus 1:5-9 (NKJV)

While the Bible adamantly sets forth explicit requirements for shepherds, it must be understood that perfect adherence to these rules cannot make a saint a shepherd. Fulfilling them to the letter of the law cannot make a saint a pastor. A person must be these things within, not without. These requirements for the ministry of pastor must be true of his heart not only of his behavior. They do not make a man a shepherd; they simply describe a man whom God has raised up to be a shepherd.

> **Outward adherence to Biblical qualifications does not make a person a true shepherd. It's an inner matter of heart.**

THE NEED FOR SHEPHERDS

A quick glance at the Church reveals the need of pastoral multi-tasking. God's sheep are in desperate need of care. Having come into the flock from a worldly system whose overlord was Satan, new lambs need care. Without exception, while in the world they were beaten and bruised, oppressed and abused. Although the horror and brutality of the world has been left behind, upon entering God's fold new lambs need their wounds to be healed. They need to be ministered to, cared for, and comforted. They need to be nursed and tended as they rest from their deliverance from sin and as they gain strength to walk in God's way. They need a pastor/shepherd.

New saints are not the only ones who need nurturing. As sheep grow older and more mature in the Lord, they still need constant supervision. They are never without need for care. They always need ministration and supervision of an overseer/ bishop/elder.

DAVID, THE SHEPHERD

David gave us that magnificent testimony of the Lord's goodness found in Psalm 23. Among the many ways that David is revealed as a type of Christ, his portrayal of the true Shepherd shines as a jewel.

David's greatest qualification for office is that he was a man after God's own heart. He not only continually sought and pursued relationship with God, but he also had a heart after—similar to or of the same kind as—His Lord.

When we first meet David in Scripture he is, quite literally, a shepherd of his father Jesse's flock *(1 Samuel 16:11)*.

David was a shepherd of his father Jesse's flock. From his own life's experiences, he knew how to care for sheep. When anointed into the Lord's service, he brought that expertise into God's kingdom. While his care of his father's animals is recorded in an historical sense, his care for His Father's flock was the expression of a spiritual pastor shepherding a spiritual flock. His work was of eternal value.

David didn't wait until he was on the throne to begin pastoring. He was a shepherd in the school of hard knocks wrought at the hands of Saul for many long years before he was a king. As he learned his lessons and journeyed from sheepfold to throne, the harsh measures that were dealt to him trained him and made him a man. Through these experiences, David learned what not to do as a shepherd and he never inflicted the cruelties done to him onto others.

David did not call himself into the Lord's service as a shepherd; God did (*1 Samuel 16*). In his role as pastor, **David was a shepherd of his father God's flock.** he sought out his own or gathered around himself those he was to lead (*1 Chronicles 12:23-28; 1 Samuel 22:2*). He remained in their presence whether in desert cave (*1 Samuel 22:1*) or in palace. David grew to be a mighty warrior (*2 Samuel 3:1*) and a giant killer (*1 Samuel 17:4-49*). He fought for, protected, and delivered his own from all enemies. When he won the city of Jebus (*2 Samuel 5:6-10*), he brought his own into their own land. That city is now known as Jerusalem.

David led his people but did not drive them. He was in front of them leading them forward, whether in war or in peace. He constantly provided for his own in matters of food, refreshment, and rest (*1 Chronicles 12:40; 1 Samuel 25:8*). David shared their brokenness and healed and bound the wounds of his flock. When crowned king of Judah and then declared king of the whole nation of Israel, he united his whole flock under one rule.

He gave life to his people by erecting David's Tabernacle and teaching them to come close to the Lord in a new order of praise and worship. David accomplished all of these things in love and mercy (1 Samuel 24; 1 Samuel 25:7).

There is a great need in the Church today for godly men to rise to a godly calling of shepherd. There is still a flock of God on the earth, and it needs to be governed. We must pray for those who will follow in the footsteps of David and lovingly rule and care for God's sheep.

JESUS, THE GREAT SHEPHERD

Just as Jesus is our example of the perfect fulfillment of the other ascension gifts that have thus far been studied, so too He is the completion or the zenith of the pastoral office. In fact, Scripture clearly labels Him as the archi-poimen or the Chief Shepherd (1 Peter 5:4).

Having learned of the Lord's pastoral ministry in Ezekiel 34 and in John 10, it is further described in Psalm 23. This beloved and universally known psalm acquaints all saints with Jesus' ministry as shepherd and overseer.

Oh, the joy of submitting to the shepherding of the Lord! "The Lord is my shepherd" (Psalm 23:1). He was, is, and eternally will be our caretaker. His flock lacks for nothing (Psalm 23:1). He meets its every need out of the abundance of His household; there is no need we can possibly have that is beyond His ability to fulfill.

The Lord brings His flock to lush green pastures and fresh clean waters (Psalm 23:2) for feeding, for drinking, for rest, and for refreshment. Since a sheep will not lie

Jesus is the Chief Shepherd. down unless it is unless it is full and content, the Lord's care is seen both in the quantity as well as the quality of His provision.

Jesus our Shepherd not only cures and cares for our bodies, but He restores our souls *(Psalm 23:3)*. Also, He leads His sheep and guides us, particularly in the areas or paths of right standing with the Father *(Psalm 23:3)*. If any sheep wanders from the path through error, sin, or rebellion, Jesus is there to lead him back into right relationship.

This true Shepherd also delivers His flock *(Psalm 23:4)*. Fear is unknown to a flock walking in faith. When faith is placed in Him, fear has no stronghold on the sheep and even a journey through the valley of the shadow of death can hold no terror. Jesus proves Himself to be our constant Companion and Friend, always present in time of need *(Psalm 23:4)*. With His rod and His staff, weapons of strength, He protects and governs His sheep *(Psalm 23:4)*.

Jesus does not deny the existence of enemies but shows His flock that the enemy cannot touch God's chosen without His permission. He teaches His flock to rule over their enemies by preparing banquets for His sheep in the midst of their foes *(Psalm 23:5)*. The Great Shepherd profusely blesses His sheep, full and beyond full to overflowing, with a heavy anointing of His precious Holy Sprit *(Psalm 23:5)*.

From this, saints can only conclude, as did the psalmist, that in His care—and only in His care—we are assured that goodness (delight, joy, fruit, and righteousness) and mercy (forgiveness and revival) shall be ours eternally (*Psalm 23:6*). And in Him is the promise of dwelling in our heavenly mansion forever (*Psalm 23:6*).

That is caretaking as it should be. That is pastoring in the truest sense. That is the perfection of governing by love and diligence that the Lord Jesus Christ manifested in His work as a Shepherd.

A COMPARISION

	THE GRACE	THE MINISTRY	THE PASTOR
REFERENCE:	John 21:16	John 21:16	Ephesians 4:11
SOURCE:	Jesus	Jesus	Jesus
FOR WHOM:	the saved	the saved	the saved
WHERE:	in home groups, Bible studies or local Church	in home groups, Bible studies or local Church	the local Church, nearby community or universal Church
WHEN:	as the need arises	as the need arises	as the need arises
PURPOSE:	to care for each member of the body of Christ on earth and to shepherd each into the loving arms of God in heaven		
METHODS:	• represent the Owner of the sheep • care for • know • seek the lost • protect • tend • lead • feed • provide for • heal give life to • teach • discipline	• represent the Owner of the sheep • care for • know • seek the lost • protect • tend • lead • feed • provide for • heal give life to • teach • discipline	• represent the Owner of the sheep • care for • know • seek the lost • protect • tend • lead • feed • provide for • heal give life to • teach • discipline

PASTORS: THE FALSE

"Yes, they are greedy dogs which never have enough. And they are shepherds who cannot understand; they all look to their own way, every one for his own gain." Isaiah 56:11 (NKJV)

"My people have been lost sheep. Their shepherds have led them astray." Jeremiah 50:6 (NKJV)

Perhaps the greatest need in the body of Christ today is for true shepherds to arise.

In the world, sheep, though usually meek, healthy, mild, and peaceful, constantly need attention. They need the ministrations of a good shepherd to get them healthy, to keep them healthy, and to care for them. The choice of shepherd and whether or not he is a good or a bad shepherd can literally make or break the flock.

So too, in the kingdom of God, God's sheep are sometimes docile, submitted, and maturing. At other times, they are cranky, sickly, cocky, or rebellious. They, too, need a pastor to keep them. The one who is placed over the flock of God and entrusted with its care can bring life or death to His sheep.

As with all other ascension gifts studied thus far, the counterfeit of God's truth—the sham, the false, and the fraudulent—has arisen in the ranks of those who purport to be God's shepherds. Almost as a flood tide, false shepherds have arisen and begun to rule over God's flock.

It is a sad fact that while there are many outstanding, loving, good shepherds, there are also some who are not. Not all who are elders are godly leaders empowered by the Holy Spirit. Not all who are bishops or overseers lead God's flock in kindness and firmness as they extend His care and government to it. Not all who are pastors or shepherds are led by or pattern themselves after the archi-poimen or Head Shepherd, Jesus.

BAD CHARACTER

FALSE SHEPHERDS DO NOT LOVE THEIR SHEEP: False shepherds are not noted for love. Actually, if false shepherds try to exhibit love, it is quite often love for self and position, not for their flock. Using sheep is not a sign of love. Neither are ignoring, rejecting, deceiving, manipulating, or driving them evidences of love.

Rather then love, false shepherds are often motivated by fear. They fear losing their job and their home. They fear the pressure of hierarchy and the demands of men. They fear change. They fear for their lives. They are a far cry from the example set by Jesus, who gave His life for His sheep.

FALSE SHEPHERDS ARE NOT DILIGENT: Rather than stationing themselves at the door of the sheepfold so as to be on guard day and night, false shepherds have gone off duty. Due to their lack of diligence, they do not recognize approaching predators or care if they enter the fold. Even if they do recognize such danger, they are not prepared to do anything about it. False shepherds are diligent in keeping the demands of denomination that require them to add to numbers, to increase revenue, or to build human empires. They are not nearly as diligent in keeping commands of God concerning sheep. Their work is summed up in an old nursery rhyme:

Little Boy Blue come blow your horn.
The sheep's in the meadow,
The cow's in the corn.
Where is the boy who looks after the sheep?
He's under the haystack, fast asleep!

WHAT DOES A FALSE SHEPHERD DO?

It is heart rending to compare the work of the true shepherds and the false. Generally speaking, while a good shepherd guards, guides, and governs God's flock, a false shepherd does not. Instead, he ignores them, uses them, or even destroys them.

A FALSE SHEPHERD HAS NO TRUE CALLING: Often a false shepherd is one who may have a calling to ministry, but it is not to serve God as a pastor. While a true shepherd is raised up and called as a pastor by God, a false shepherd is not.

A false shepherd may raise himself up. Perhaps wanting the position and the finances he thinks will be his as a pastor, he moves into an area, begins to draw people into his web, and then sets himself up as the leader of a "church."

In addition to such pride or greed, ambition may call the uncalled into ministry. These false pastors work to serve themselves and to fulfill personal dreams. Often they are driven by a desire to be important. If their motives were seen through and put down or ignored in the world, they then decide to be somebody in the Church. They study for ministry and often end up as pastors. Rather than dealing with their problems, they just change locations, gravitate from world to Church, bring their problems, ambitions, and failures into the Church, and play out the game. With no call of God in their hearts and no anointing of God in their lives, they proceed to manipulate, control, and enslave the sheep.

Some false pastors are raised up by family. It is all too common that some whose father or grandfather was a minister come under intense pressure to keep ministry a family tradition. The weak will give in and do all that is required to become pastors.

The ministry of pastoring is not hereditary.

Other false pastors are raised up by people in positions of responsibility. Some may have attended Bible school, and upon graduation they were prematurely given a local Church to tend, even though they had no life skills or experience. These have become the tool of a particular denomination, and they begin doing as they have been labeled—they pastor. More on this later.

At a deeper level, sometimes Satan will raise up his agent to assume control over God's people. Whatever the source of his "calling," this false pastor, a product of rebellion, does not know God's will and doesn't acknowledge that God has any say in his life.

A FALSE SHEPHERD ACTS FOR HIMSELF: A false shepherd does not understand that although the sheep are his in responsibility, they are not his in ownership. He doesn't see that he is accountable both to them and to God for them. Shortsightedly, he does not see the sheep as the flock of God but sees himself as the god of the flock.

A false shepherd does not view himself as one who is charged to exercise the government of the true Owner of the sheep. He does not comprehend that he is only a representative of God who is to extend the kingdom of God among God's people on earth. Instead, he considers himself to be the owner with every right to extend his own rules and his own kingdom. Rather than rule or govern righteously, he tyrannizes ruthlessly. In truth, he is not a shepherd but a despot.

> A false shepherd does not see sheep as the flock of God but sees himself as the god of the flock.

A FALSE SHEPHERD STEALS SHEEP: If a true shepherd will search out his flock (*Ezekiel 34:4*), then a false shepherd will not. A false shepherd will not recognize the limitations placed on him by God but will rebel against them. He will not acknowledge that there is one flock to which he is called. He wants all the sheep, not just some of them. He is not satisfied to seek out and minister only to those whom the Lord has designated as his.

Since this false shepherd is not anointed by God he will not follow God's orders. He will not seek out his Master's sheep but rather will search for a flock to call his own. He won't accept the sheep intended as his but will search for others who can add to this numbers, who fulfill his own dreams, and who will make him look good.

God is the overseer of families in both the world and the Church. Whether by His perfect choice or by allowing their rebellion, God oversees a man's and woman's relationship and marriage. Usually, He blesses them with offspring of their union. These parents and children form a family unit. The father is the head of the family, and he must search out, keep, and govern his particular family.

Even if parents are not satisfied with the family God gave them, even if they disagree with Him concerning the sex, number, or talent of their offspring, they are not allowed to go raiding other families to trade or steal their children in order to add them to their own family. They must learn to be content with those they have been blessed with or those who God chose to be their own.

In the Church, a false pastor does not recognize this principle. Whether for reasons of ego or because he is constantly under pressure by his denomination to increase his flock, numbers become all-important to him. He is forever passing the sheep under his rod to count them *(Jeremiah 33:13)*. If the sum of them is judged deficient, rather than shepherding the ones he has, he spends much time and effort looking for and luring those someone else has. In his desperation to assuage his ego or get his hierarchy off his back, he is not too selective in his methods of inducing sheep to join his flock.

> **A false shepherd robs the sheep of other shepherds.**

Since a false shepherd wants a bigger flock, he will actively engage in raiding neighboring flocks, enticing unstable or greedy sheep with empty promises to get them to come into his field. Ignoring his own sheep who need to be cared for, he decimates godly flocks and leads those sheep to strange pastures. He simply will not be content with his flock as it is nor let God give the increase.

Worse yet, he often teaches his sheep to be a part of his nefarious scheme. He instructs them and expects them to participate in his "membership drives," perhaps through clandestine phone calls inviting the unwary to Church events, through false word of mouth bragging, or through enticing their children to "better" youth programs. The price the false shepherd pays for unlawfully adding to his flock is that he becomes the governor of a flock just as ambitious, rebellious, and ignorant as he is.

A FALSE SHEPHERD DOES NOT REMAIN WITH HIS FLOCK: Although a true shepherd stays with his flock (*Ezekiel 34:8*), a false shepherd will not. Unlike the false shepherd just mentioned who tries to coerce sheep to leave their proper flock and join his, sometimes it is the false minister who tries to leave his flock.

As any true man of God knows, at the local Church level no one can be a long-distance pastor. This includes pastoring regularly via television, skype, email, twitter, and CD. It is only a false shepherd who would ever imply that he could personally shepherd God's sheep via electronic communication. A true shepherd is with his sheep, not in a TV studio or on a computer hundreds (or thousands) of miles away from his flock. While apostles, prophets, evangelists, teachers, and those in the ascension gift of pastor can very effectively minister via television or radio, it is impossible for shepherds with the grace or ministry of pastor in the local Church to care for, tend, or govern that way. If there is no constant communication and direct contact with sheep, there is no true pastoring.

A false shepherd will spend much time away from his flock. He constantly rejects it, sometimes abandoning it completely. Instead of raising up and releasing other saints in his flock to go out to minister, he all too often goes himself, leaving his sheep unattended. Time after time, he is not there to care for them when emergencies arise or life's changes demand guidance.

Often this false shepherd will simply use his Church as a springboard to bigger and better things. Keeping all the perks of office such as building, parsonage, salary, and titles, he rejects his flock and goes out to promote himself. He is not married to his flock but to his ego and ambitions.

Soon a vicious cycle sets in. His flock, not understanding or liking this callous treatment, reacts with resentment and soon begins to decline. Indifferent to the cries of the uncared for sheep and unwilling to expend more time and care on them while his eyes are on greener pastures, the false pastor then leaves.

The final indignity is that if a call to a new church does come to this false one (or more accurately, a false calling of his own choosing), he will not release the flock he so despises. Wanting to control them but not to love or care for them, he will not let them go even as he himself moves on. He pretends to befriend and advise the new pastor, then finds and exploits his weak spots, and brings the new pastor under his iron grip too. Thus, from where ever he may be, he perpetuates the love-hate relationship.

A FALSE SHEPHERD WILL NOT SEEK THE LOST: While a true shepherd will look for those of his flock who are lost or scattered, a false shepherd is the one who scatters the flock (*Jeremiah 23:1-2: Ezekiel 34:5-8*). Often he does so by physically abandoning them. Just as sheep without shepherds will scatter or wander from their flock, so too people without leadership will wander about but go nowhere.

Also, a false shepherd scatters sheep by neglect. If hurts are not cared for, healing and deliverance are not sought after, burdens are not lifted, then sheep, hoping for greener grass on the other side of the fence, will wander away. In desperation to get their needs met, they will leave their own field and flock and go elsewhere.

Rather than seeing his own faults or negligence and repenting of them, a false shepherd will just let the scattered sheep wander and fall away. Rather than admitting and confessing his own sins of rebellion, disobedience, and neglect, he will blame the sheep for all the wrongs they have suffered, leave them separated from the flock, and allow them to be fresh meat for wolves. Refusing to take responsibility for his massive role in their destruction, the false shepherd will pronounce judgment that the sheep got exactly what they deserved.

Those false shepherds who have so miserably failed in their duty to bring unity to God's flock are directly accountable to God for that failure. Any false shepherd who has presided over the ungodly breaking up of a local Church or the dissolution, separation, or falling away of the body of Christ from God has placed himself under holy judgment. Woe to false shepherds who scatter the sheep!

A FALSE SHEPHERD WILL NOT PROTECT HIS FLOCK: While a true shepherd will deliver his flock out of the hand of the predator, a false shepherd will not. He will not protect them *(Ezekiel 34:8)*. A false shepherd does not truly care about his sheep, and, all vocal protests to the contrary, he simply does not think they are worth risking his own life over.

God's sheep need protection in many areas. The thief comes among them to steal, kill, and destroy (John 10:10). One thing that he is determined to steal from God's sheep is their blessings.

One such blessing is their reward for obedience. A false shepherd will suppress sheep that God is raising up to service or leadership positions in a local Church. Perhaps feeling a threat to his own supremacy, a false shepherd will oppose and squash any other ministry. In such a way, he robs God's sheep of both the blessing of obedience and the victor's crown.

A second way sheep are robbed is in tithing. God has commanded that His people are to honor Him by offering a tithe. Often sheep are agreeable and even eager to do so. They want their money used to spread the good news and to build the kingdom of God on earth. Then along comes a false shepherd with ideas of his own as to where the tithe should go. He proclaims false prophecies, dreams false dreams, and shares false visions. Suddenly, the gullible sheep are building their pastor's kingdom, not God's, expanding his empire, not God's, or supporting and financing his word, not God's. When the land is bought, the building built or expanded, and the plaster dust settled, the sheep were robbed of the blessing of the riches of eternity and placated with a temporal temple. When false shepherds have preached false dreams and forced the sheep to finance them, when they have robbed the flock of their blessing, the term fleecing the sheep takes on a whole new meaning.

Hear the Word of the Lord, false shepherds:

The LORD stands up to plead, and stands to judge the people. The LORD will enter into judgment with the elders of His people and His princes; "For you have eaten up the vineyard; the plunder of the poor is in your houses. What do you mean by crushing My people and grinding the faces of the poor?" says the Lord GOD of hosts. Isaiah 3:13-15 (NKJV)

False shepherds also rob sheep of leadership. They do not protect God's lambs nor lead them to safety. If thieves of truth come over the wall of the fold and into the flock, they allow it. If robbers steal sheep, they permit it. If predators come, they do not stand fast but stand aside and let them into the fold. All too often the false shepherd not only fails to protect his sheep but is, in fact, the predator. It is he who leads his lambs to slaughter.

A FALSE SHEPHERD WILL NOT KEEP HIS ASSIGNED PLACE: If a true shepherd leads his sheep to their own land, the special place intended for them, then a false shepherd will not. A false pastor will carve out his own place or his own empire. Since he is in rebellion against God and will not acknowledge His authority, he has his own ideas of where he will lead the flock. He will take the sheep to a land but it isn't the land God meant them to have. Simply stated, a false shepherd will lead sheep to the land or place of his own choosing for them, not the land of God's choice.

> **A false shepherd will not accept any limitation on the scope of his ministry.**

Some false shepherds have grown up within the Church system and are familiar with Church routine and purposes. Rather than God's will, they will only promote denominational goals and doctrinal intents. By failing to break out of man-made and man-ordained aims, they do not lead the sheep to God's ground.

Other false pastors may have their own ideas on where they want to go and how to use their sheep to get there. They may set their own goals or dream up things they want to see achieved. These goals, aims, and uncharted seas are in no way what is best for the flock, nor do they bring the flock into its own place in God's plan. They simply stroke the ego of the false overseers.

A truly false shepherd will forego all boundaries, trample on all limitations, poach, and encroach in order to realize his dreams. In blind ambition, he will use the sheep to build his empire but not to build God's. This false shepherd is ambitious and unrestrained.

A **FALSE SHEPHERD WILL NOT LEAD:** A true shepherd will lead his flock; a false shepherd will not (*Ezekiel 34:8*). In leadership, a false shepherd fails in two areas. First, out of fear, he does not lead at all; rather, he holds back. Perhaps through ignorance, laziness, or jealousy, he holds his sheep back. Denying that Christianity is an on-going journey which always seeks to advance to new ground, a false shepherd keeps his sheep in the same field endlessly seeking food which has long since been overgrazed. He simply keeps the same flock in the same meadow until they starve, fall ill, and die from lack of food.

Or, a false shepherd will not lead his flock but will drive them. In fear, he will not go first and lead the way. Rather, in cowardice, he will beat his sheep and force them to go on ahead of him to see if the path is safe. If it is, he will follow and then take all credit for the advance.

Once he has the basics of coercion under his belt, he will go on to learn the art of control, not of leadership. He will have his nose in everyone's business and his finger in every pie. He will call this meddling ministry.

Rather than primarily being concerned with caretaking, he will expend all his energy controlling. Like the worst taskmaster in Egypt, he will endlessly and ruthlessly crack his whip over his sheep. His dreams must become reality; his empire must be built.

As surely as the Hebrews were slaves in Egypt, many saints are slaves in the Church. To add insult to injury, the slave-saints are commanded, as were the Hebrew slaves, to sing songs to their tormentors, to pretend they feel joy, and to keep up a show of well being (*Psalm 137:3*).

False pastors oversee the flock in fulfilling their own ambitions. They drive the flock in a downward spiral until it is trapped in forced labor. They gird their flock in chains, enslave it, and force it to do their bidding. False shepherds don't read the Scripture that commands them to:

"Tend—nurture, guard, guide and fold—the flock of God that is [your responsibility], not by coercion or constraint but willingly; not dishonorably motivated by the advantages and profits [belonging to

the office] but eagerly and cheerfully. Not (as arro-
gant, dictatorial and overbearing persons) domi-
neering over those in your charge, but being exam-
ples—patterns and models of Christian living—to
the flock (the congregation)." 1 Peter 5:2-3 (TAB)

A FALSE SHEPHERD DOES NOT FEED HIS FLOCK: While
a true shepherd feeds his flock *(Ezekiel 34:2-3),* a false
shepherd will not. Instead, he starves them. Although he
may know of several good pastures where food or the
Word of God may be found, he may neglect to lead his
sheep there or command them not to go there by themselves.

A false shepherd limits his sheep in the quantity of
food he allows them. Although sheep should be given a
constant diet of the Word of God, those driven by an ungodly slave driver have little food to eat. As earlier stated,
often they are only allowed to nibble at already overgrazed pastures where no nourishment exists.

In addition to the limited quantity of good food, a
false shepherd will also neglect the quality of the food he feeds his sheep. For the
sheep of a tyrant there are no such things
as lush, green meadows. His sheep receive no supplements and don't know
anything about a balanced diet.

A false shepherd starves his sheep.

For many sheep, the pure Word of God is adulterated
by the impure word of the false shepherd. He feeds Scripture to sheep according to his own interpretation of the
Word, or force-feeds them denominational doctrine.

Perhaps even more damaging to the flock than in-humane starvation is the reality that the false shepherd no longer cares for the flock; he only cares for himself. Though a false shepherd neglects to feed the flock, he never forgets to feed himself *(Ezekiel 23:2-3)*. Taking all the fat or best parts of the food, he always ensures that his own needs are met.

A FALSE SHEPHERD DOES NOT QUENCH HIS FLOCK'S THIRST: A true shepherd will lead his sheep to water, but a false shepherd will not *(Exodus 2:17)*. Just as a false shep-herd's feeding procedures are inadequate, so too are his thirst quenching ones. Sheep on the move need water to live. Jesus is life- giving water. From Him flow streams of living water. In Him is refreshment and relief from thirst and drought. Unfortunately, a false shepherd's sheep are rarely rather than constantly brought to Jesus. If they do not receive from His eternal spring, there is no relief in their thirst for Him.

A FALSE SHEPHERD WILL NOT ALLOW HIS SHEEP TO REST: A true shepherd will see that his sheep rest. For sheep under the "care" of false shepherds, there is no such thing as rest.

False shepherds are always driving their flock and do not know the meaning of the word rest. Those who are not true spiritual leaders do not know or recognize rest and are therefore unable to lead their sheep there. In-stead, with no direction from God, they constantly strive to achieve by forcing "their" sheep to accomplish the false shepherds' personal dreams, goals, and ambitions by works of flesh. No matter how badly their flocks need physical or spiritual rest, they view any attempt at rest as treachery or rebellion. Under such false shepherds, the dreary become weary; they soon stumble and then fall away.

A FALSE SHEPHERD DOES NOT HEAL: A true shepherd will care for his sheep's health needs. A false shepherd will not (*Ezekiel 34:4*). A shepherd is charged to get his flock into a healthy state and to maintain it there. False shepherds not only don't do that, they are often the cause of the health problem.

Sheep under stress tend to get sick. Underfed, undernourished, underwatered, exhausted sheep tend to get sick. Health quickly breaks down when ruthless methods and unending demands are practiced on sheep.

After breaking down the health of a once hardy flock,

A false shepherd wounds rather than heals.

a false shepherd has no idea how to heal his people. First of all, the false shepherd will not acknowledge that he is responsible for poor condition of his flock. Because of this attitude, he does not repent of his actions or intercede on behalf of his diseased and ailing saints. Second, a false shepherd can't be bothered with nursing duties. If he goes to visit the ill or weak, he often whisks in with a "let's get this over with" look on his face, slaps some oil on the head of the hurting one, utters some unintelligible words and breezes right back out.

If the hurt or wound or disease is in the spirit of the victims rather than in the body, a false pastor's ways are even more brusque and brutal. Not knowing much about spiritual healing and often denying that the need for deliverance even exists, he not only will not but also cannot meet God's requirements for the care and spiritual healing of his sheep. Covering up his ignorance or lack of care with interrogation ("How could you be sick? We believe in healing in my Church.") or accusation ("Your faith must be weak—if you only believed, you'd be healed!"), he does not heal, bind, or mend. Instead, he hurts, wounds, and breaks.

A FALSE SHEPHERD BRINGS DEATH: As a true shepherd brings life to his flock, a false shepherd does not. Since a false shepherd represents self, man, or Satan, his ministry does not focus on Jesus, the Author of life. In no way does he express holiness, joy, health, love, or kindness that are the essence of Jesus Christ and the mainstays of His life. Truly reprobate shepherds express and manifest the attributes of the opposite master, Satan, the prince of death.

A FALSE SHEPHERD DOES NOT TEACH TRUTH: In addition to care, saints need teaching. A true shepherd takes the greatest of delight in instructing God's sheep about their Lord, but a false shepherd will not.

A false shepherd's failure to adequately nurture and tend God's flock is reflected in his failure to properly teach. He may adulterate the pure Word by adding his own; he may erroneously interpret Scripture and teach error; he may deny the whole Word and only present only the parts with which he agrees. He may neglect entirely to introduce new lambs to the Christian way of life or deny older sheep aid in their walk. If truly reprobate, his most serious offense may be that instead of teaching God's Word, he may introduce a whole new word, the doctrine of demons.

False shepherds lure new converts by introducing enticing, exciting, personal revelations rather than by instructing them from the Bible. Their classes on basic Christian principles are sometimes little more than fundamental brain washing advocating a questionable personal or denominational stance. The false pastor's personal beliefs or preferences become the main emphasis of the teaching, even outstripping Jesus Christ as the chief topic of instruction.

Of course, the Church is of great importance to the saint but only as long as it is in submission to its head, Jesus Christ, and not to an ungodly man or hierarchy. If denominations aggrandize their doctrines, and if false pastors, for fear of losing their jobs, do as they are told and concentrate their teachings on man's church and its man-made doctrine instead of on Jesus as Savior, Lord, King, and Head of the Church, the result is error. If these faulty practices are not changed, instead of teaching sheep truth and leading them to life, they will be encased with lies and ultimately may be led to death.

A FALSE SHEPHERD WILL NOT DISCIPLINE HIS FLOCK: Finally, while a true shepherd will engage in disciplining his flock, a false shepherd will not. In a total mockery of leadership, he looks out over an abused, neglected, uncared for, and ill-taught flock and sees problems and rebellion—yet he does nothing.

Perhaps a false shepherd knows that the excesses of his own abuse will not allow him to point his finger at another. Perhaps he is ignorant of the disciplinary processes of the kingdom he claims to represent. Perhaps he's too fearful or has no stomach for internal squabbles. Whatever the reason, the final indignity that a sheep has to suffer is that she cannot be helped or protected by the disciplinary process. Her own shepherd refuses to separate the sheep from the goats *(Matthew 25:32)*.

False shepherds fail to realize that God disciplines His children as an expression of His love for them *(Hebrews 12:6)*. They do not admit that the love they are supposed to express to the sheep does not rejoice at injustice and unrighteousness *(1 Corinthians 13:6)*. Nor does it cover up injustice and unrighteousness.

The one who refuses to discipline sheep is a false elder. The one who allows sheep to wander off and foment trouble in other flocks is a false bishop. The one who sees sheep in error and rebellion and allows them to stay there is a false overseer. The one who refuses to call sheep to accountability is a false pastor. The one who, for whatever reason, will not acknowledge when the horizontal covenant between saint and saint has been breached and who ignores all rumblings and warnings of trouble until disaster destroys the flock is a false shepherd. His sheep eventually reflect his own weaknesses and failures.

LEVELS OF FALSE PASTORS

1. **THE UNANOINTED:** This might be the person who, while bumbling through life, suddenly finds himself a pastor. He may be one who genuinely wanted to shepherd sheep but had no divine call or holy anointing to do so. In going ahead anyway, he arrived in a dead end job, had no ability to care for or teach those given into this care, had no desire to govern, saw no fruit after years of toil, and quickly got burned out. Somewhere along the line this disillusioned, tired man gave up his ambition but not his position, and he still ineffectively gathers the remnant of his just as hopeless flock each Sunday morning to go through the motions of "Church."

2. **THE EMPIRE BUILDERS:** The next level of counterfeit ministry in pastoring concerns the self-appointed who seek to build their own empire. Since they have no calling or leading from God, they do not know what they are doing and therefore do not do it well. They are a product of flesh, and so they work in the flesh to fulfill their own dreams and build their own houses rather than fulfill God's vision for the Church. Their headship is not Christ but themselves, man, or denomination. Their work does not glorify God but themselves, man, or denomination. They are not led by the Spirit, but by themselves, men, or denomination.

3. THE REPROBATE: Yet there is yet a far worse type of false pastor. This is the truly reprobate shepherd. These are the false pastors who don't care for the sheep but instead destroy or scatter them. Rather than loving God's flock, they hate it. Instead of caring for it as unto God, they control it as unto their god, Satan. Their work reflects the ideals of their master and extends his government and kingdom on earth.

DOEG, THE FALSE SHEPHERD

As David was a living example of a shepherd after God's own heart who cared for and ruled his people well, so Doeg is his antitype, the shepherd who destroyed the flock. Doeg was the chief of Saul's shepherds (*1 Samuel 21:7*). He was present when David, escaping from Saul's murderous rages, went to Nob and asked Ahimelech, a priest, for food and weaponry before fleeing to the cave of Adullam.

When an enraged Saul inquired after David, Doeg **Doeg destroyed the priests of God.** betrayed David. Doeg also betrayed Ahimelech and the priests of Nob and caused them to be brought before Saul. And, when Saul's own guards would not do so, it was Doeg who, *"turned and struck the priests, and killed on that day eighty-five men who wore a linen ephod"* (*1 Samuel 22:18 NKJV*).

There are two sad lessons to be learned from this incident in history. First, Doeg was not a Hebrew. He was an Edomite (*1 Samuel 18:22*). That means that he, one who was not a member of God's flock, was in charge of God's flock. Today, are there not pastors who aren't even believers, yet who are shepherding God's sheep?

Second, if a truly false shepherd (whether a believer or not) is in charge of a Church, he is often the very one who turns on the sheep, lashes out at them, and destroys the very saints who are the priests of God in the New Testament Church *(1 Peter 2:9)*.

WHY?

If forced to walk in his flock's shoes, a false shepherd would never allow himself to suffer the same maltreatment that he inflicts on his own sheep. Therefore the question must be asked: why does the false minister act as he does? Why does he torment God's flock?

WRONG VIEW OF WHO HE IS: Although distantly acknowledging that all pastoral ministry ought to be based on the pattern set by Jesus, who was the Good Shepherd, false ministers often forget that Jesus was also the Lamb of God. Thus, many false shepherds forget that they too are sheep. They do not realize that they are a part of the very flock they are abusing. They do not know that everything they are doing unto others they are also doing unto themselves.

LACK OF QUALIFICATIONS: Some false shepherds fail so miserably because their qualifications are so sparse. While the Bible is meticulous and thorough in its descriptions of true shepherds, false shepherds and Pastoral

Search Committees within the Church system often overlook them, negate them, or make up their own. When they then appoint someone to be a pastor who isn't able to care for their flock, they seem surprised that he turns out to be a false pastor.

PROBLEMS WITH PRIDE: Another erroneous belief that influences a false pastor involves pride. The thoughts of some candidates for ministry lead them to disaster. Some false shepherds believe that the sole eligibility for pastoring is the degree they have received from Bible school. They think that their man-taught, man-earned degree has readied them or totally equipped them to minister. They believe that a piece of paper which denotes intellectual success in a prescribed course of studies has fully qualified them for or takes precedence over God's call to pastoring.

False shepherds place undue importance on human credentials. A piece of paper, no matter how well earned, does not make someone a pastor. False pastors, eager to put down any threat to their job or title, will mock and despise those God has called but who lack formal training. They will aggrandize themselves because they have a degree or a diploma.

False shepherds forget that though Jesus did not go to Bible school or hold a degree He was called by God to do a work. Empowered by the Holy Spirit, He did so in wisdom and competence. Would any dare demean Jesus' intelligence? Would any dare say that the perfect Shepherd was lacking in any respect?

Surely a working knowledge of the Bible is essential to anyone given the office of pastor. However astonishingly as it seems to some, God did not make graduation from Bible school with all of its pomp and ceremony, its degrees and title, a primary qualification for office. Only man has done that.

PROBLEMS WITH THE BIBLE SCHOOLS: In addition to lack of qualification and wrong mindsets, another problem concerning false pastors sometimes stems from the Bible schools themselves. Bible schools can train and educate minds, but they don't often create wisdom and grace. Nor do they often grant sustained, in-the-field experience to young people who have been confined to classrooms and who have been primarily concerned about projects, papers due, or upcoming exams. Degrees earned may testify to intellectual success, but mental studies do not completely prepare students to fulfill a spiritual office.

A true elder is one who holds a position of authority based on maturity as well as intellect. His experience has been gained over a period of years, not by a quick jaunt through Bible school. Graduating at the top of the class does not grant him wisdom or a caring heart. Those come from God, grace, and experience, not from books. Green graduates of Bible schools are by no stretch of the imagination prepared to be elders. Rather than seeking a Church to pastor, a better course would be to go into a local Church and submit

Most graduates from Bible school lack experience.

to established, godly leadership for extensive on-the-job-training.

Another problem found in some Bible schools is that, year after year, they churn out young people that they **Many Bible schools wrongly label all of their graduates as pastors.** claim are qualified for ministry. Almost indiscriminately, they label their green graduates as pastors. Whether the young person's gifts are as prospective apostles, prophets, evangelists, or teachers or whether he has a ministry gift of the Holy Spirit that he can use to bless a local Church, graduates are not called ministers (which all saints are), but pastors. They are called such, treated as such, and counseled to consider themselves as such in seeking the leadership of a Church within the Church system.

The fact that some Bible schools do not teach that all ministers are not pastors and therefore do not, can not, **All Bible school graduates are not pastors.** and should not function as such has caused abuse in both the ministry and the Church! From the graduates' point of view, how many fledgling apostles are confined to the responsibilities of pastoring a local congregation when they should be submitted to an apostolic team in order to learn to succeed in overseas ministry or to build new churches? Or, how many teachers want to grow in the Word but because someone labeled them a pastor, they are forced to spend all their time caring for a flock instead of teaching it?

Concerning the effect on the Church, how many local Churches have had to endure in a "pastor" the indifference of a missionary openly awaiting his call to the foreign field? Or, how many have had to put up with the constant din of salvation messages being shouted to an already saved flock or enduring absentee leadership since their pastor is really an evangelist whose heart takes him to the unsaved?

How many ministers masquerading as pastors use a Church, gobble up its money, and exhaust its people for lack of a better way to spend their time? How many abandon the flock they felt forced to oversee without a backward glance and leave the Church in shambles when something better comes along?

Rather than continuing to mislabel, misdefine, and misdirect its graduates, Bible schools should honestly seek the Lord's direction for each one of them. They should treat them as who God says they are.

Again, upon graduation, ministers should submit to the local Church rather than try to lead one. They should not lead true elders but learn from them. In so doing, a missionary, rather than caretaking in frustration, could be helping the Church at the same time he is preparing himself to go abroad. An evangelist could assist a local Church yet be free to go where necessary whenever necessary without needing to also spend countless hours preparing sermons or organizing Church life. A teacher could freely pore over, study, and glean from his Bible and books and present instruction on the Word to the Church without the pressure of overseeing the body as well. Then, when the call came for any of these to leave the local Church and go to another area to minister, their abrupt departure would not leave the Church in rudderless disarray with no continuing leadership or authority.

All ministries of the Church are necessary, integral parts of the Church, but not all ministries or ascension gifts are that of pastor. True ministers will leave pastoring to the pastors. False ones will not.

FALSE PASTORS WORK UNDER THE LEVITICAL PRIESTHOOD

A final problem in allowing Bible schools to assume the authority to raise up pastors is that these they often churn out graduates who have been trained in the ways of the Levitical priesthood and they therefore keep the Church under ritual and law.

To explain, 3,500 years ago God released the Hebrew children from bondage in Egypt and then met with them at Mount Sinai. He made a covenant with them, gave them the Ten Commandments, and set down some laws and ordinances. Then God gave Moses both directions for building the tabernacle and commands concerning a special group of men called priests who would minister there.

These priests honored Aaron, brother of Moses, as their first High Priest. This priesthood, ordained and initiated by God, placed the priests between man and God. All action from the people toward God had to be through a priest. When the Hebrews wanted to offer gifts or sacrifices for purposes of dedication, thanksgiving, communion, or reconciliation with God, everything had to be done for them by a priest. Essentially, the Old Testament priest became a middle-man; the correct order of worship was man, priest, God.

This God-ordained priesthood served God in a certain, set, prescribed manner. Exact conformity to God's rule and law was mandatory. Any deviation or violation of the order or ritual, however small, was regarded as a grievous sin and an abomination in the sight of God.

This ritual, regulation, and liturgical observance soon turned into religion and tradition. Worship of God was accomplished through ritualistic slaughter of animals whose shed blood covered man's sins and reconciled a sinful people to holy God.

The Levitical priesthood became bogged down in rules and regulations.

This priesthood remained in place for fifteen hundred years. When it became bogged down in rules and regulations, not only the ones the Lord had given, but also the ones the people had added, it could not function properly. It raised traditions of man to new highs and debased the commands of God to new lows. It promoted acts and works of flesh and denied the validity of the Spirit of God. Slowly, through tradition, rebellion, and the corruption of the priests themselves, this system brought slow death instead of life to the people it served.

This type of priesthood may sound familiar to saints and servants of God today. It is the priesthood that remains in large parts of the Church today. And, unhappily, this is the type of priesthood that some Bible schools both promote and teach their students to be a part of.

Those Bible schools still train their fledgling pastors to be middle-men and to expect the flock of God to totally depend on them. Bible schools and their graduates aggrandize the pastor, make them high priests of the local body of Christ, and imply that the way to God is through them. They believe and teach that all Church responsibility lies on their shoulders and that they are in total charge of the Church without anything but token help from the saints.

Those Bible schools do not realize nor teach that this emphasis on one-man ministry reflects a traditional, ritualistic priesthood that has long since been replaced. They don't understand that it is a part of a system that often functions in flesh, not in spirit, and it thereby denies the glory and sovereignty of God. They don't acknowledge that this system keeps pastors religiously working to follow Old Covenant form. They don't see that it keeps saints, who aren't restricted to the Old Covenant and its ritual of law but who were given the New Covenant and are under its Spirit, in a house of death.

But they do wonder why it all goes wrong.

The truth is that the Lord Himself declared the end of this Old Covenant priesthood two thousand years ago. When Jesus died on the cross, the Levitical priesthood was finished.

The change from Old Covenant to New ushered in other changes too.

A CHANGE IN HIGH PRIEST: First, there was a change in the high priest. The high priest was no longer to be a descendant of Aaron from the tribe of Levi; the new high priest was to be after the order of Melchizedek. The High Priest of the New Covenant is Jesus *(Hebrews 7)*.

In being both priest (by offering sacrifice for the sins of the people) and Paschal Lamb (by being the sin offering which was sacrificed), Jesus became the High Priest of the new order. In Him, New Testament believers have not a temporary High Priest but an eternal One. His works are not fleshly and imperfect but are wholly holy and perfectly perfect.

A CHANGE IN WORSHIP: Second, as the High Priest changed, so did the order of worship. Under the Levitical priesthood, animals were endlessly sacrificed to atone for sin. This was a type or shadow of the coming sacrifice of the true Passover Lamb, Jesus.

When Jesus died, His one sacrifice was so perfect and complete, it never had to be, indeed could not be, repeated or done better. His own words concerning the sacrifice were, "It is finished." *(John 19:30 NKJV)*.

When Jesus died as the perfect sacrifice for sin there was never again a need to sacrifice another animal. This made the primary work of the Levitical priesthood obsolete. From that point on, God set forth a new order of worship. He commanded the new priesthood to worship Him in a different way. While there was no longer to be animal sacrifice, there was to be the sacrifice of praise. While God's priests were no longer to ritualistically, silently involve themselves in works of flesh, they were to loudly, joyfully, musically worship Him in Spirit and in truth.

A CHANGE IN PRIESTS: Finally, just as the High Priest and the focus of the priesthood changed, so did the priests themselves. When Jesus died, the veil in the temple was torn in two from top to bottom. This signified that access was given or the way was made for all saints to enter the Holy of Holies to worship God. The priesthood changed in composition from one small, exclusive group of specially sanctioned men from the tribe of Levi to all New Testament saints, both men and women, who call Jesus Savior and Lord. *(1 Peter 2:9; Revelations 1:6).*

A CHANGE IN COMMUNICATION: When the order of priests changed, the order of communication with God changed too. It was no longer man, priest, God, but saint (who is priest), Jesus, God. Through Jesus, the High Priest, each saint has access to the Father.

A CHANGE IN SERVICE TO GOD: Saints are no longer to expect or to wait for others to worship for them or to allow another person to control their relationship with

God. They are to get on with serving God themselves. Saints are no longer to expect or look for their priest or pastor to be their middle-man. Saints are to do the work of ministry (Ephesians 4:12) while pastors and other Church leaders are to care for, rule, teach, and discipline them as they do so.

Without question, God has raised some saints to places of leadership. Jesus has given some to be pastors for the equipping of the saints for the work of ministry and for building up the body of Christ. However, it is also without question that these leaders or pastors should act as shepherds and overseers, not as Levitical priests imposing ritual and law on their flocks.

THE FRUIT OF THE FALSE PASTOR FOR HIMSELF

Just as the results of abuse have wounded the Church, the effects on the pastors themselves also have been devastating. Beating sheep does not come without a price.

It is a fact that God lays the blame for apostasy in the Church squarely on the shoulders of the false shepherds who would not go to seek the sheep who were scattered (Jeremiah 50:6). He also places blame on the false pastors for the saints who have been devoured by demonic hoards (Jeremiah 50:7; Ezekiel 34:5-8).

Since God is a holy God who cannot look on sin, His demand for justice must be satisfied. While He gives all men a time for repentance, a day of reckoning is coming.

> *Thus says the Lord GOD: "Behold, I am against the shepherds, and I will require My flock at their hand; I will cause them to cease feeding the sheep, and the shepherds shall feed themselves no more; for I will deliver My flock from their mouths, that they may no longer be food for them."* Ezekiel 34:10 (NKJV)

Tormented sheep are going to be delivered from the hands of false shepherds and false shepherds are going to pay a price for their evil. False shepherds are without excuse. They have seen Jesus as both the Good Shepherd and as the Passover Lamb. Through the Word they have seen the perfection of Jesus in His service as pastor and seen the results of effective pastoring in the meek, gentle, wonderful Lamb of God.

However, they have ignored Him. They have rejected His ways. They have instead chosen to become wolves, expressing the care and character of their true master, Satan.

In days of old, God judged another who had abused the house of God (*Daniel 5*). Belshazzar, ruler of Babylon, was partying and lording it over his people rather than caring, governing, teaching, or disciplining them. He openly abused God's house by commanding that the holy vessels that had been taken from the temple in Jerusalem be brought for use in his debauchery. As he drank and caroused and praised his man-made gods, a disembodied hand appeared and wrote on the wall of his house. Understandably, this terrified him, and he called for an interpretation

Daniel told Belshazzar that he (Belshazzar) had not learned from the past (*Daniel 5:22*), that he had abused vessels meant for the God's service (*Daniel 5:23*), and that he had praised false gods while ignoring the one true God (*Daniel 5:23*). The handwriting was a word of judgment: **MENE MENE TEKEL UPHARSIN** (*Daniel 5:25*). Thus Belshazzar was told that his reign was finished, that he was found wanting, and that his kingdom would be divided. He died that same night.

The same story is told today. God has placed vessels in the house of God, anointed saints who were to be used honorably in His service (*2 Timothy 2:20-21*). Instead, they have been mocked, humiliated, and, in some cases, made a part of unholy festivity.

Just as surely, the handwriting is now appearing on the walls of many a church and parsonage: **MENE MENE TEKEL UPHARSIN.**

The judgment: false pastors have not learned from the past. They have been found to be in rebellion to God. They have abused God's chosen vessels. They have praised and submitted to false gods who build human kingdoms and empires while ignoring true God and His kingdom. They didn't measure up. They have been weighed on the scales and been found wanting.

THE FRUIT OF FALSE PASTORING ON THE CHURCH

Too many shepherds have not biblically guarded, guided, or governed the Church since Jesus left the earth many years ago. The results of such negligent pastoring have been disastrous. The ramifications of the problem run so deep and spread so wide that it is hard to imagine the whole horror.

ABUSE: The first bad fruit of an ineffective pastoral system is abuse. The Church has brought many into its buildings with well intentioned promises of care. It has taken in many who were physically and mentally abused in the world system, and then, instead of healing their hurts and delivering them from evil, it has seen false shepherds further traumatize them. Some lambs have been so brutalized that they have never fully recovered.

CONFUSION: A second result of poor care is confusion. False pastors who have steadfastly refused to exercise authority have lost it. With a loss of authority comes a corresponding loss of direction. False pastors and sheep alike are milling around going nowhere.

STUPOR: Third, with no true shepherd to help them, some abused lambs of God enter a stupor. Saints' senses are dull and their minds and spirits are blank. They've become so desensitized by constant exposure to trauma that to survive at all, they have locked themselves into tradition. They are seen ritualistically performing their duties and alter what should be a living relationship with

God into a religious exercise in the hope that some day it will all get better.

REBELLION: A fourth negative result is that a large group within the Church system has gone their own way. With no godly governing or management, with no caring or training, they have been reduced to doing what is right in their own eyes. Some have had enough, have taken matters into their own hands, and have begun to do their own thing. They are no longer content to play Church, and they are trying to minister without knowing how. The Bible refers to this as rebellion.

APOSTASY: Rebellion has led to further problems. Much of the Church is now in apostasy. What began as a small trickle has become an angry torrent of sheep leaving the fold.

GOD'S GLORY IS GONE: Perhaps the most devastating result of abuse by false pastors is that the glory of God has departed from much of that which calls itself the Church. In days of old, because of corruption, evil, negligence, and despising the presence of God, the Ark of the Covenant was taken from its rightful place, brought into battle, and lost to the enemy. When the Ark was taken into captivity, Ichabod, which means the glory of the Lord has departed, was declared as a judgment over the land. One of the most tragic truths of the whole situation is that the Ark had been abused and wrongfully transported not by ignorant soldiers but by the evil priests, the false spiritual leadership of the day (1 Samuel 4).

So today, it is the false priests and pastors who have tried to put God in a box, taken Him where He did not say to go, and, in so doing, have brought judgment and the loss of His presence to many.

OUR RESPONSE TO THE FALSE PASTOR

DISCERN: Saints need to ask, what must we do about this problem of false pastors? First and foremost, saints must discern (*1 John 4:1*). They must humbly seek God in fasting and in prayer. They must judge the spirit of a pastor and look at the fruit of his ministry. They must discern if it brings death or life. They must determine whether it represents the Levitical priesthood or follows after the ways of Jesus. They must ascertain if its primary goals are to increase numbers, raise revenue, and build empires, or whether they are caring, overseeing, teaching, and disciplining God's children. Saints must evaluate the situation in their local Church, determine if it meets God's standards and, if it does not, ask themselves why they are there.

REPENT AND CONFESS SIN: Second, all sheep must repent and confess their sins unto God. While great fault lies with the false shepherds, it also lies with the passive sheep. All priests of God must approach the true Shepherd and ask forgiveness for their sins concerning false shepherds.

Saints must confess as sin the fact that in many ways they have perpetuated the system to which they fell victim. They must confess every instance when they refused to accept or to work in the job God gave them to do and instead left it in the hands of the pastor (which forced him out of the caring role into other fields of ministry to which he was neither suited nor called).

Also, saints must repent and confess that they have not followed God from Old to New Covenant. Although there was a time when God clearly ordained a Levitical priesthood, those days are gone. Today, since the priesthood has changed, so must the priests.

Saints must confess their sin of religiously following after unholy tradition.

Finally, saints must repent of allowing evil to continue. They must confess that apathy has perpetuated a false priesthood and that, without a bleat of protest, they have allowed its presence. They must acknowledge that complacency has caused them to be silent lambs even while being led to slaughter. They must admit laziness in which they have not matured and so sat idly by while evil became entrenched and then enthroned in God's body.

BELIEVE: A third thing that saints must to in order to right this horrible wrong is to believe the truth.

Jesus knows the wretchedness of His saints. He too was abused by a religious system. He too was led like a lamb to the slaughter (*Isaiah 53:7*). He too has suffered as saints do. He too has been where saints are. Out of that suffering He has brought great victory.

Saints must believe that God has heard the heart cries of His lambs for release from bondage. They must not doubt that He will act on their behalf. They must have faith that He will deliver His sheep (*Ezekiel 34:10*). They must know that God is going to deal with this situation (*Jeremiah 25:34*).

God is raising up true shepherds (*Jeremiah 3:14-15*). He is going to send to His sheep servants, both old and young, who have a true shepherd's heart. He is going to anoint twenty-first century Davids, people who will keep their Father's sheep (*1 Samuel 17:34*). He will raise those like David, who withstood Saul, a type of the false Church system. God is going to send elders, leaders, and shepherds who will bring the power, presence, and glory of God back to the remnant of the true Church.

Saints must see the new dawn. They must know the trumpet of God is sounding. Saints must rally around Jesus Christ, the True Shepherd of the sheep. They must remember and recite the scriptural promise given to them:

> *Behold, the Lord GOD shall come with a strong hand, and His arm shall rule for Him; Behold, His reward is with Him, and His work before Him. He will feed His flock like a shepherd; He will gather the lambs with His arm, and carry them in His bosom, and gently lead those who are with young. Isaiah 40:10-11 (NKJV)*

Saints must know that Jesus will yet show His tender heart and extend His sure mercies to His repentant flock and that He will express to them His unending and perfect love.

PASTORS

	THE TRUE	THE FALSE
CHARACTER:	• love their sheep • diligently care for their sheep	• do not love their sheep • do not diligently care for their sheep
PURPOSE:	• guide, guard, and govern the flock of God • minister life, truth, community, care and God's love to God's Church	• substitute a false church base on the Levitical priest hood and the Old Testament temple worship • tear down and destroy the true Church by abusing and confusing the saints • apostasy
LEVELS:	**THE GRACE:** those enjoying caring for people that they oversee in a small group; • those whose hearts lead to greater expressions of love to the saints in a local Church	• bumblers who find themselves in the position of overseer, • aren't qualified, but won't give up their position of control over God's saints
	THE MINISTRY: pastors who genuinely care for and love the flock given into their care	• the self-appointed intent of building their own empires
	THE SHEPHERD: elders, bishops, overseers, and pastors who guard, guide, and govern the saints of God as pastors to pastors on a universal Church level	• the agents of Satan intent on destroying the Church and God's saints

METHODS:	• have a true calling • acknowledge God as the owner of the sheep • acknowledge God's limits as to the makeup of their flocks • remain with their flocks • seek those who wander • protect their sheep • lead their sheep • feed their sheep • lead their sheep to water • allow their sheep to rest • heal the hurt and wounded • bring life to their sheep • teach the truth • govern and discipline	• self or satanically appointed • act like the sheep are theirs • acknowledge no boundaries in increasing their flocks - rob sheep of other shepherds • will not stay with their flocks • will not seek the lost from their flocks • will not protect their sheep • will not lead their sheep • will not feed their sheep • will not lead their sheep to water • rest is considered as rebellion • will not heal • bring death to their sheep • will not teach or teach lies • can't govern and will not discipline

TEACHERS: THE TRUE

"And He Himself gave some to be...teachers."

Ephesians 4:11 (NKJV)

From Scripture we learn that one last ascension gift has been given to the Church for the edification of the body of Christ and for the perfecting and maturing of the saints. That is the teacher (Ephesians 4:11).

In the Greek, the word for teacher is *didaskalos*. A godly teacher is one who is acquainted with Scripture and who then interprets it or instructs other saints concerning it in matters of Christian doctrine and faith. He is one who digs into, ascertains, and then presents the truths of the Word. He is one who clearly, simply, succinctly, and boldly exposes the truth as found in Scripture.

To some, the ascension gift of teacher is included in that of pastor. To others, it is a separate, though interrelated, ministry. In this writing, since a part of a teacher's function is distinctly different than that of a pastor, the gifts will not be treated as one, that of pastor-teacher, but as two, both pastor and teacher.

To differentiate briefly between pastor and teacher, one of the prime qualifications for the ministry of pastor is that he must be able to teach. However, not all teachers are required to be pastors. Also, a pastor cares for and governs his flock as well as teaches it. A teacher, on the other hand, confines his work to instruction in Scripture.

A second contrast of teachers with pastors shows that a teacher introduces the basic tenets of Christianity to the flock of God and then expands upon them. He lays down or instructs in great detail the scriptural truths which are the foundation stones of godly faith. He teaches in order to excite a way of learning. A pastor, on the other hand, takes those basic, foundational principles and extends them or amplifies them by applying them as holy principles in daily living. He preaches in order to encourage a way of life. Another way to say this is that a teacher applies himself to reaching the mind of a saint, while a pastor concentrates on reaching his heart. A teacher teaches and then a pastor teaches and preaches in order to reach the saints.

GOOD CHARACTER

The character of a teacher must be above reproach. Since he is warned that a teacher receives a stricter judgment (*James 3:1*), he must be a man of the highest faithfulness and virtue. He must not be the lackey of a particular denomination but a saint of honor. He must not be a dispenser of false doctrine, but a disciple of justice and truth.

A true teacher is a righteous and mature person. He is in right standing with God. Since he is responsible to deal with babes as well as more mature Christians, he cannot be a person who would lead others into error. Soundness and integrity must be his hallmark.

WHAT DOES A TEACHER DO?

Without question, whether introducing godly doctrine and true principles of Christian faith or whether endeavoring to incorporate them into Christian life, the basis or foundational source for all teaching is the Word of God. The Bible says: *"All Scripture is given by inspiration of God, and is profitable for doctrine, for reproof, for correction, for instruction in righteousness"* (2 Timothy 3:16 NKJV).

From this Scripture, it is possible to see a double function in the use of God's Word for instruction. For those who will gladly hear and respond to godly teaching, the Word instructs in righteousness and lays out doctrine. For others who have been wrongly taught or who are willfully following a wrong way, it is also the basis for reproof and correction. Any word, book, pamphlet, or instructional tool that contradicts the Word of God is invalid as a means of teaching about God. Likewise, any work or teaching which adds to or takes away from His holy Word or which presents an additional or "new" revelation based on questionable denominational theology is anathema in the eyes of God (*Galatians 1:6-8*).

Good teachers work from facts. They investigate and then expound on biblical truth. In the world, any good researcher is charged to learn the who, what, where, when, how, and why of any situation before he can accurately report on it. Just so, since a teacher of God must spend much time in investigation or searching out biblical fact before he can teach what has been learned, this same questioning process can yield much fruit in learning more about teachers and teaching.

WHO: First of all, who are those in need of teaching? From Scripture, we learn that men are to be informed (Matthew 5:19) and that women (Jeremiah 9:20) and **A true** young women (Titus 2:3-4) are to be **teacher** taught. So also, all children are to be in- **teaches** structed (Deuteronomy 4:9). Further- **everyone.** more, people (Ezekiel 44:23) and nations (Matthew 28:19- 20) are to be taught. Since all saints fall into one or more of these categories, all saints must receive biblical education.

However, sinners also must be enlightened. The Bible states that sinners and transgressors must be tutored in His ways *(Psalm 51:13)*.

WHAT: The Word of God proclaims what needs to be taught. A quick glance at a concordance indicates a multitude of topics. For instance, the Word urges instruction in wisdom *(Job 33:33)*, in the fear of the Lord *(Psalm 23:11)*, and in numbering our days *(Psalm 90:12)*. It calls for tutoring in knowledge *(Isaiah 28:9)*, in the will of God *(Psalm 143:10)*, in Jesus Christ *(Acts 5:42)*, and in His ways *(Colossians 1:28)*. It expresses a need for learning about war *(Judges 3:2; 2 Samuel 22:35; Psalm 144:1)* and about holiness *(Titus 2:12).*

Furthermore, through the ages saints have asked for instruction in various areas. Saints in other times and places have cried out to God to teach them His ways *(Psalm 27:11; 86:11),* His paths *(Psalm 25:4),* His statutes *(Psalm 119:12),* His good judgments *(Psalm 119:66),* and how to do His will *(Psalm 143:10).* Perhaps most familiar is the plea or the heart cry of New Testament disciples in asking Jesus to teach them to pray *(Luke 11:1).* Shouldn't twenty-first century saints be crying out to be taught the same things?

WHERE: Since we know who is to learn and what is to be taught, we must determine where the instruction is to be done. Quite simply, all teaching must be done within the Church. Godly teachers work in and of the Church, not in and of the world *(Acts 13:1).* Although all saints were once in the world and taught its ways by its overlord, Satan, those worldly teachings are not applicable to, desired by, or justified in believing saints. From the moment of their salvation experience, saints must learn and obey the ways of their new Lord and Master, Jesus Christ, and of the kingdom of God. They do so through the truthful interpretation of Scripture by godly teachers in the Church.

A true teacher teaches anywhere, anytime.

All teaching focusing on God must proceed from God's earthly seat of authority, the true Church. All teachers must be a part of and in submission to a local Church. Whether they function at the local or universal levels, there cannot be proper instruction to or about the house of God apart from the house of God.

However, please do not mistake the intent of these words. Bearing in mind that the Church is not a denomination, a place, or a building but a people who believe in and obey God, a teacher can teach in almost any situation. For example, since the Lord is present where two or more are gathered in His name *(Matthew 18:20)* as well as everywhere at once, a teacher can instruct very small groups as well as very large ones.

Just as a true teacher has no limit on the numbers he can reach, so he is not bound by location. Many teachings may take place in more formal settings like classrooms or the Church's sanctuary. However, even though Jesus often taught inside in the synagogue, He was just as often found outside on mountainsides, by the seashore, on dusty roads, and in gardens instructing His disciples. Therefore, Jesus' present day teachers also are free to accomplish their instruction in the beauty of His creation as well as within the confines of a Church building. Further, as a teacher moves from local Church to universal Church, he may find himself presenting scriptural truth in large lecture halls, via electronic communication such as tape, radio, television, or Internet.

Biblical instruction does not always have to be in the same place at the same time to be effective. In the first century Church, teachings moved from house to house (Acts 20:20). If today's homes are a part of the local Church is it any less appropriate that teachings should take place in them? The main requirement for a teacher is that he present the truth of God within the boundaries of true Church doctrine and within the limitations of the authority of Scripture.

WHEN: In questioning when to teach, a teacher instructs whether in a preplanned schedule or whenever the need or the occasion arises. Observing the caution to be ready in season (2 Timothy 4:2), a teacher is always prepared to expound on the Word. Teaching is an on-going process.

HOW: The focus or main point of all teachings is the Lord Jesus Christ. Every book in the Bible relates to Him, discusses Him, portrays Him, or prophesies about Him. The Old Testament contains the message of His coming, while the New Testament depicts His life both leading to and after the cross. Since Scripture, the source of a teacher's instruction, magnifies Christ, so should all teaching. If Jesus authenticated Scripture as a source of learning and used it to teach of Himself (Luke 24:27), so all teachers should follow His example and do likewise.

The focal point of all true teaching is Jesus. Good teachers do not center their teachings around man, their own ministries, an unbalanced topic, or denominational doctrine. Instead, their whole focal point is Jesus. A good teacher can instruct on endless topics and yet stay within the guideline that all teaching must relate to and manifest Christ.

Further, a true teacher is one who presents a systematic course of instruction *(Luke 24:27)*. For example, he can teach about a particular book of the Bible, such as the gospel of Luke. In so doing, he will spend long hours dissecting that book chapter by chapter and verse by verse until those under his instruction have a working knowledge of the facts and principles therein. Or, an instructor can select a certain topic such as healing, tithing, or the Sermon on the Mount. Then, using Scripture as his source of knowledge, he will confine his instruction to issues involved in that topic and show how they pertain to Jesus and the whole Word of God until students arrive at an acceptable level of knowledge concerning it.

In addition to being systematic, good teaching is progressive *(Matthew 5:2-11)*. A true teacher does not teach and reteach just the elementary doctrines of Christ. Rather, he presents them as foundational principles and then moves on *(Hebrews 6:1)*. Nor does he delve into one topic and stay there forever. Rather, he presents a balanced instruction of the whole of Scripture.

Also concerning progression, a good teacher's work has a forward thrust. His aim is not just to bring understanding of the Word but also to promote growth in using it. Good teaching is accompanied by practical application that will produce in those who listen and learn the desire to be doers of the Word and not hearers only *(James 1:22)*.

Also, a teacher must teach publicly. As Jesus did, so must His disciples do (*Matthew 4:23; John 18:20*). Teaching in private can lead to error and confusion. Partial or faulty understanding of good teaching can lead to problems. It is the wise teacher who presents his instruction publicly so that all things can be checked and verified (*Acts 17:11*).

Finally, concerning a teacher's methods, a godly teacher often instructs from biblical fact that has become reality in his own life. In that sense, he teaches from experience.

In the world, a teacher must know the subject he is teaching. He must have a greater grasp of the facts and principles than his students do. He cannot instruct in areas where he is not knowledgeable. Just so with God's teachers. They must thoroughly know their topic. Head knowledge is not enough. There must be the reality of the topic in their hearts as witnessed by the fruit of it in their lives. Godly teachers must live what they teach, the visible product of a life spent with the Lord.

Living the Word gives teachers the ability to then instruct the Word. Teachers cannot successfully teach about love if their attitude is hateful. They cannot train disciples in belief if they walk in doubt. The hypocrisy of instruction in praise and worship would be evident if the instructor does not engage in either. Nor could spiritual warfare be successfully taught unless the one teaching it knows his subject, has been involved in it, and has emerged in victory. The bottom line is that the most effective teachers have come to know about God both in His Word and in His school of life (*2 Timothy 2:2; John 3:11*).

WHY: As for the whys of teaching, the label provides the motivation: a teacher teaches. He is concerned with raising disciples of God. Believing that knowing the ways of God will lead saints to be obedient to them, a good teacher will teach tirelessly in order to promote discipleship.

Also, a godly teacher knows that Christian life cannot be lived without truth (*John 4:24*). Since teaching springs from the Word that is truth and presents Jesus Who is the Way, the Truth, and the Life (*John 14:6*), all Christian reality is based on and requires truth.

Pilate once asked, "*What is truth?*" (*John 18:38 NKJV*) **A true teacher presents the Truth.** when the Truth was standing right in front of him. The deepest motivation of a true teacher's heart is to search out and present truth so that others will not be as short sighted as Pilate was. He presents truth so that saints know in Whom they believe.

As a final motivation, a teacher's goal is to train and instruct others, some of whom will then become teachers (*2 Timothy 2:2*). In this way, the gift goes on.

LEVELS OF TEACHERS

1. THE GRACE: This is when a saint is anointed by God to teach a particular subject in a particular place at a particular time. It may happen only once or occasionally, but if the saint is prompted by God, it is a genuine expression of teaching *(Luke 12:12).*

2. THE MINISTRY: The second level is a true teacher of God's Word in the local Church. This is a person with a ministry of teaching who has first been taught and who then teaches others *(Titus 1:9).* If his teaching becomes known, he may be asked to teach at other venues in his Christian community.

3. THE TEACHER: This is the true teacher who, while under submission to a local Church, is raised by God to leave that body and go out to function or instruct in the universal Church. This is the person described in Ephesians 4:11 as having the gift of teacher.

HOW IS A TEACHER CHOSEN?

The authority for all teaching comes from the Godhead. It is God alone who raises true teachers *(John 3:2).* Jesus is authorized to train them and send them out *(Mathew 28:19-20).* The Holy Spirit is the active agent of teaching, the one who teaches the teachers *(Luke 12:12; John 14:26; 1 Corinthians 2:13).*

GOD'S JEWELER

A godly teacher can be compared to a jeweler who has great treasures in his possession. Rather than limiting himself to just one kind of treasure, he displays a whole spectrum of jewels, the whole Word of God. He examines his jewels and carefully learns all he can about them. Realizing the value of them and wanting to share their beauty, he displays his treasures tastefully and honestly. He understands that he must, at the right time and in the right way, share his pearls of great price. Similarly, a true teacher learns all he can about the Word of God, and then he shares his pearls of wisdom and truth.

JESUS, THE TEACHER

Surely by now it is evident that there is no more supreme example of a teacher in Scripture than Jesus Himself. As with all other godly ministries, He is the zenith of the teaching gift. He was recognized as a teacher *(John 1:38; 3:2)* and went about all Galilee teaching *(Matthew 4:23)*.

Jesus authenticated the Old Testament as a valid source of knowledge concerning Himself and revealed how it pertained to Him *(Luke 24:27)*. Through His earthly life and teachings, Jesus laid the basis for New Testament Scriptures to be written of Him. His instruction included such things as the kingdom of God *(Mark 10:13-16)*, good fruit and bad *(Matthew 25:14-28)*, righteousness *(Matthew 5:6,20)*, and sin *(Luke 18:9-14)*. Jesus also raised others to do the same *(Acts 8:12)*. In His teaching, He introduced God's disciples to the will of God and commanded them to follow it. Above all, He Who was Truth presented truth.

Jesus taught about Himself and God's kingdom.

APOLLOS, THE TEACHER

To show that people could successfully function as true teachers, the Word leaves us the record of Apollos. He was a cultured and eloquent man who was well-versed and mighty in expounding the Scriptures (Acts 18:24). He had been taught and with great zeal he, in turn, instructed others (Acts 18:25). The main point or focus of his teaching was Jesus (Acts 18:25). Scripture portrays him as a man both diligent and truthful in his task (Acts 18:25), and fearless and bold in his style (Acts 18:26).

This teacher was also teachable. When he understood the need for further learning in his own life, he submitted **Apollos taught and was willing to learn.** to others for additional instruction (Acts 18:26). So successful was Apollos in presenting the truth of God and the ways of the Lord that he left the local synagogue (with its blessings) and taught in the universal arena (Acts 18:27). He was of great help to Christians in teaching them to refute old ways and bondage to the law by teaching them the absolute truth that Jesus was the Christ (Acts 18:28).

Would that God would send the true Church many more Apolloses!

A COMPARISON

	THE GRACE	THE MINISTRY	THE TEACHER
REFERENCE:	2 Timothy 2:24-26 Matthew 28:19-20	2 Timothy 2:24-26 Matthew 28:19-20	Ephesians 4:11
SOURCE:	Jesus	Jesus	Jesus
FOR WHOM:	for all	for all	for all
WHERE:	not bound by location	not bound by location	not bound by location
WHEN:	in season	in season	always
PURPOSE:	instruct all about their Savior, Jesus Christ	instruct all about their Savior, Jesus Christ	instruct all about their Savior, Jesus Christ
METHODS:	clearly, systematically, knowledgeably use the Word of God to instruct about Jesus and His kingdom	clearly, systematically, knowledgeably use the Word of God to instruct about Jesus and His kingdom	clearly, systematically, knowledgeably use the Word of God to instruct about Jesus and His kingdom

TEACHERS: THE FALSE

"And in vain they worship Me, teaching as doctrines the commandments of men." Matthew 15:9 (NKJV)

It would be wonderful to believe that chicanery has not invaded the ascension gift of teacher. However, that would be inconsistent with Satan's pattern of interference and disruption in his attempts to pervert, and therefore nullify, godly ministry. The sad truth is that in order to keep the true Church from being built and to keep its saints in bondage and immaturity, Satan has assaulted all Church ministries with sham and fakery. Just as the spiritual government of the apostle, prophet, evangelist, and pastor are rife with the ungodly and the counterfeit, so too is that of the teacher. Thus, the ungodly counterpart of the true teacher of God is the false teacher.

BAD CHARACTER

As for character, the false teacher has none. He knows nothing of integrity. He is not a righteous instructor of the righteous God but rather a base person full of pride. He is ignorant and has a fondness for disruption and dissension (*1 Timothy 6:3-5*). His very being is corrupt. An indictment against false teachers is found in the first book of Timothy:

> If anyone teaches otherwise and does not consent to wholesome words, even the words of our Lord Jesus Christ, and to the doctrine which accords with godliness, he is proud, knowing nothing, but is obsessed with disputes and arguments over words, from which come envy, strife, reviling, evil suspicions, useless wranglings of men of corrupt minds and destitute of the truth, who suppose that godliness is a means of gain. 1 Timothy 6:3-5 (NKJV)

WHAT DOES A FALSE TEACHER DO?

Since much was learned in asking the questions who, what, where, when, how, and why of the true teacher of God, it would be wise to apply these interrogations to the false teacher also.

WHO: In addressing the who of false teaching, it must be ascertained both who is a false teacher and also who is falsely taught.

Concerning the first of these, false teachers are often found within the Church. In Jesus' day, he labeled Pharisees (*Matthew 19:3*), Sadducees (*Matthew 22:31*), and scribes and elders (*Matthew 15:1-9*) as false teachers. Surely then it should be no surprise that some Church leaders today may fall into that same category.

In addition to false teachers within the Church, there are false teachers without. These false teachers have not accepted Jesus as Savior and do not acknowledge Him as Lord. They who teach about a Lord whom they do not know and a Church of which they are not a part. Scripture aptly describes them as the blind leading the blind.

Concerning who is falsely taught, false teachers don't care who they teach. Ministers in the flesh are eager to reach anyone they can in order to present their version of the truth, announce their own unlearned, unscriptural opinions, and promote their own name and ministry. They are not choosy about what they present or to whom they present it.

The truly depraved false teachers also try to reach a universal audience. They prey not only on the unwary and undiscerning in the Church, but they also attach themselves to sinners in the world and lead them further astray.

The Church must acknowledge that everywhere it looks it sees those who are hungry and thirsty for knowledge of the true God. Therefore, it must raise and authorize holy teachers to draw the lost with truth, to answer questions honestly, to provide a sound basis for Christianity, and to staunch the outflow of compromise to denominational or outright erroneous doctrine.

False teachers are both in and out of the Church.

At the same time that it is providing the truth, the Church must stop the enemy from presenting his lies. Although false teachers' intent is to gobble up the unsuspecting, God's justice is going to require them to account for every saint who was led astray and for every sinner who was devoured through poor or erroneous teaching.

WHAT: Next we must find out what false teachers teach. In one word, the answer is lies.

Already it has been discussed that false teachers teach sectarianism. They instruct in denominational doctrine or one particular group's theology. They don't teach the whole Word of God but only that part of it which favorably relates to or promotes their own church's point of view.

Additionally, false teachers involve themselves and others in "....*foolish controversies, genealogies, dissensions and wrangling....*" *(Titus 3:9 TAB).* They instruct about irreverent legends, godless fictions, tales, and silly myths rather than of Jesus Christ *(1 Timothy 4:7).* They exploit their listeners with cunning but false arguments *(2 Peter 2:3).*

Further, rather than letting the Holy Spirit determine the topics of instruction, false teachers teach what their listeners want to hear *(2 Timothy 4:3).* For instance, false teachers might endlessly drill a congregation about healing, finances, or the easy life since that is what will keep them in the limelight or keep their listeners' attention.

False teachers realize that saints have their own goals and expectations. Right or wrong, these saints will attend teachings that tell them what they want to hear or which are aimed at their field of interest. To gather a following, false teachers will pander to people's desires. They will not teach what God or the true Church leadership wants presented but that which tickles the ears of their listeners. With no thought of obedience to God or submission to His authority, their motivation is to flatter and to placate other people.

Also, false teachers promote the adherence to or return to law and bondage. They instruct on the traditions of men (*Matthew 15:1-9; Mark 7:1-9*) rather than in the freedom of God. They dwell on the letter of the law rather than on the law of the Spirit of life in Christ Jesus (*2 Corinthians 3:6; Romans 8:1-2*). As if that isn't enough, the truly reprobate go on to introduce a contrary gospel with its associated heretical doctrines. We are warned:

> I marvel that you are turning away so soon from Him who called you in the grace of Christ, to a different gospel which is not another; but there are some who trouble you want to pervert the gospel of Christ. But even if we, or an angel from heaven, preach any other gospel to you that what we have preached to you, let him be accursed. *Galatians 1:6-8 (NKJV)*

> But there were also false prophets among the people, even as there will be false teachers among you, who will secretly bring in destructive heresies, even denying the Lord who rought them, and bring on themselves swift destruction. By covetous-

ness they will exploit you with deceptive words.
2 Peter 2:1,3 (NKJV)

WHERE: Continuing with our interrogation, we must learn where false teachers will be found. Scripture tells us that they are found both among the people in the world and in the Church. False teachers attack the unsaved as well as the saved. In any setting, they present their master strategy and grand plan. They counterfeit and mimic truth, perform as learned sages, draw the unwary with pretense and make-believe, and spring a death trap on them.

Perhaps they start by finding the loners or strays either in God's flock or in the world. As soon as they spot, isolate, and befriend the weak, they begin the process of introducing error.

False teachers also invade home groups. It is without question that Church cell groups are divinely sanctioned. However, home groups with no adequate leadership or godly supervision are not. Home groups which have no biblically knowledgeable, mature saints among their members are an invitation to disaster. It is often to these that false teachers come or from them that they arise.

There are also small groups that do not meet with the knowledge of or under the authority of the Church. Some are composed of the genuinely hungry and thirsty who aren't seeing their needs met; others are made up of the malcontents who are in rebellion. In either case, without knowledgeable supervision, it is only a matter of time be fore trouble begins.

Last to be addressed is the public media. Concerning personally proclaimed teachings, just because a person goes from local Church to universal Church in his teaching does not mean that his work should not be checked and rechecked for accuracy. Moving into a larger arena of presentation is no guarantee of infallibility. Errors can still be made. National or international exposure is no assurance of truth; in some cases it is just a bigger chance to teach a lie.

Concerning the printed media, often inaccurate and misleading articles, magazines, and pamphlets purporting to be authentic teachings of God are distributed over a large area. All too often publishing houses do not check them for biblical accuracy. Printing and publishing to some is no more than a big business whose ultimate goal is profit, not instruction. Not knowing or perhaps not caring that they are disseminating misinformation, the only books that these companies are really interested in are their ledgers. False teachers are neither denied access to the public nor corrected as long as the sale of their material keeps the money flowing in.

A similar situation exists in the electronic communications industry. Many in the worlds of secular radio, television, the Internet, or the recording industry do not know the Word of God. Therefore, they cannot identify or define error. If paid to do so, they will put on any program that seems religious to them even if it is rife with error.

Similarly, communications companies owned or operated by religious organizations do not always present the truth. The companies sometimes present programs that teach about denominational doctrine, their own theology, or one point of view rather than the whole Word of God. Often they promote a particular ministry rather than the One to whom they are supposed to minister. Additionally, it seems that although they claim to be Christians, they too allow programs highlighting questionable teachings from questionable sources, ministries, or teachers if the price is right.

Realizing that their words aren't going to be too closely checked by those whose only motivation is to make money, false teachers are quick to exploit the situation. They step into the public arena, pay to have their messages publicly transmitted, and deceive more and more people. Then, in a twist of irony, they make enough money from the undiscerning to pay their bills and keep their false ministry flowing.

However, there is one bill or account that is coming due that they can't pay. Those who have earned the description of *"....men of corrupt minds and destitute of the truth, who suppose that godliness is a means of gain"* (1 Timothy 6:5), will soon find that God has opened His accounting ledgers. They are going to discover that they are accountable to God for what they have cost others and what they owe Him.

WHEN: Concerning the when of false teaching, counterfeit instructors engage in their evil at all times. Satan,

**False teach-
ers are always
preying on
the unwary.**

like a roaring lion, is always on the
prowl looking for those whom he
may devour (*1 Peter 5:8*). So are his
henchmen. Satan is no easy taskmaster. He doesn't give days off or
paid vacations. He endlessly and mercilessly drives his
minions and cracks the whip on the slow-to-obey. He is
always training and sending out false ones, and he always
expects that they will produce error and evil or they will
answer to him. He never rests nor allows his false teachers to do so either. He commands his followers to lie and
deceive whenever they have opportunity to do so.

HOW: To some extent, the how of false teaching has
already been covered. False teaching is not necessarily
systematic. It doesn't present the whole truth that should
be thoroughly taught until it is thoroughly learned. Instead, it skips around here and there, lighting on and then
abandoning topics. This lack of in-depth study keeps the
teacher of flesh from displaying his ignorance, and it can
give anyone the appearance of a sage. The Bible describes
this flighty approach to teaching:

> ....*so then, we may no longer be children, tossed
> [like ships] to and fro between chance gusts of
> teaching and wavering with every changing wind of
> doctrine, [the prey of] the cunning and cleverness
> of unscrupulous men, [gamblers engaged] in every*

shifting form of trickery in inventing errors to mislead. Ephesians 4:14 (TAB)

On the other hand, if a false teacher does teach systematically, if he does at length teach on one topic, all his listeners should be aware that it is nothing more than a systematic presentation of error.

Nor is false teaching progressive. In its insistence on placing people back under the law it does not proceed from death to life but from life to death.

False teaching doesn't move in an upward or onward direction. It does not cause spiritual growth. It keeps saints focused on books, charts, and tests. It never gives them practical application nor sends them out to test their wings.

Learning is only complete if it is useable. It is only complete if it can be successfully applied to life. If it is not applicable and life changing, it is only head knowledge and therefore often useless.

WHY: Finally, we must learn why false teachers do what they do. Although they do try to control the Church by their selection and duration of teaching and they do try to make a profit by the presentation of error to mass media, their ultimate motivation is far more nefarious. The final goal of a false teacher is to deny Christ (*2 Peter 2:1*) and thereby to usher in the antichrist.

God is Truth; Jesus is Truth (John 14:6); the Holy Spirit is the Spirit of Truth (*Hebrews 10:29; John 16:13*). It is the goal of false teachers to deny that, and, in both small groups and large, present man, denominations, or false gods as truth.

False teaching denies the true Godhead and raises up false gods. In turn, these present rosy pictures of what

False teachers seek control and introduce the antichrist. they can do for man. They encourage and preside over the spectacle of saint and sinner selling themselves to whomever seems like the highest bidder or what appears to be the best deal. False teachers let the wavering hear what they want to hear. They patronize and support the unwary and give them what they want. They portray God's demands as harsh and advise their listeners to go where the living is easy. False teachers instruct their listeners to defy the call to obedience when rebellion is so popular. They warn against abiding in the truth and provide a comfortable setting where lies predominate. In all this seduction from truth, soul after soul is led from Savior to slaver, from Christ to antichrist.

LEVELS OF FALSE TEACHING

1. THE IMMATURE: The first false teacher is the person who, with every good intention, is yet in error and is harming the Church body through his false teachings. He may be one who has been prematurely thrust into the position of teacher. Then, in his scrambling around for a topic or knowledge, he finds false training that, in ignorance, he presents to his students as truth. Too, he may have physically left a particular denomination but not spiritually cleaned his own house. Therefore, he is teaching old half-truths along with the true Word. Or, he may simply but unwittingly be the tool of someone who has control of him, and so, right or wrong, he does as he is told (*1 Timothy 1:7*).

2. THE SELF-PROMOTER: A second level of error involves the false teacher who works to promote himself. He presents his own thoughts and speaks by his own authority. His teaching comes from himself, and he seeks his own glory (*John 7:18*).

This false one prepares and presents his lessons in the flesh. No holy power falls on them and little or no fruit results from them. He functions with no godly anointing.

He may arise within the local body by tooting his own horn, raising himself up, and placing himself in a teaching position. He may feel that he is an unheralded martyr who must tell the Church truths that God has revealed only to him. On the other hand, he may be a rebellious know-it-all who conducts unauthorized Bible studies in homes or at work without the Church's blessing or even without its knowledge.

Or, he may have been placed in an influential teaching position by a desperate pastor who had no one else to turn to. Then when this false teacher's true colors begin to show and error begins to invade the Church, that same pastor, if he doesn't know Scripture very well, doesn't recognize error or doesn't think it's enough of a problem to address so he doesn't correct it. He has created a situation that he is unable or unwilling to terminate. In either case, flesh rules, and the Church, bound and led by error, is in trouble.

3. THE REPROBATE TEACHER: If ego drives the teacher of flesh further amiss, or if Satan deliberately introduces one of his own agents into teaching positions, false teachers and their teachings become demonically inspired *(1 Timothy 4:1; 2 Peter 2:1)*. The false teacher becomes a wholly unholy teacher, a pawn of Satan. If this is hard to believe, remember that it was the serpent himself who first introduced and taught lies and deception to God's children all those many years ago in the Garden of Eden *(Genesis 3)*. He is still doing so today.

DIFFERENCES BETWEEN TRUE AND FALSE TEACHERS

There are many differences between true teachers and false. Many of these differences are caused by lack of training, study, or expertise in the word of God.

FALSE TEACHERS DON'T KNOW THE WORD: First, while a true teacher may have obtained several degrees and may know a lot of facts, he does not truly know the Word of God. From such sources as books, media, ministry, classes, and seminars, he may know about the Word. He may often quote what others tell him about the Word. Rarely, however, will he personally know the Word in truth or in depth.

FALSE TEACHERS DON'T USE THE WORD AS THE PRIMARY TEXT FOR TEACHING: Second, a true instructor of God uses the Word of God as the primary source and authority for his teaching, but a false teacher will not. Since he has not truly learned the Word, he will not teach from it either. He cannot give what he does not have.

A false teacher of flesh will not dig out and present truth from the Word. Stopping far short of that, he presents truth as he sees it, as he thinks it is, or as he would like it to be. Or, rather than using God's Word, he falls back on human resources (what he has read or heard or been taught by someone else), and, without checking the authenticity or the accuracy of these resources according to Scripture, he uses them anyway. In short, he presents the word of man.

Ungodly false teachers deny that it is the Word that edifies (Acts 20:32). They neither acknowledge Jesus' own authentication of the Old Testament as a valid instructional tool (Matthew 4; Luke 24:27) nor honor His statement that Scripture cannot be broken (John 10:35). Further, when truly into false teaching, they deny the relationship between Christ and the Word. They deny that Christ is the Word (John 1:1; Revelations 19:13). They then persist in futile efforts to teach God (or their god) without the Word or to teach the Word without God. It cannot be done. Finally, they may teach what they claim to be God and His Word that is really an unholy, demonic substitute in disguise.

> **False teachers don't know or instruct from the Word of God.**

FALSE TEACHERS DO NOT TEACH THE WHOLE WORD OF GOD: A third problem with false teachers is that they do not teach the whole Word of God. They only teach that part of the Word that pertains to their personal views or those of their denomination. In so doing, they are often found teaching the commandments of men (*Matthew 15:9*).

Long ago, Jesus laid the foundation for the one true Church. He left one set of rules that were found in His Word to guide and govern it. Rather than admitting that Christ is the Head of the Church (*Ephesians 1:22*), man has divided God's Church into dozens of denominations and hundreds of churches. Each has its own basic doctrine and theology. In turn, these separate groups have raised up teachers who are then asked to present to saints of like persuasion the denominational version of truth. Instead of correctly teaching the whole Church the whole Word about God, they present just one small part of the whole that represents their own beliefs or "proves" their point of view.

In effect, teachers can become false teachers by limiting God's Word to man-made theology. Armed with denominational manuals and sectarian syllabi, they demote God's Word as the true teaching authority and substitute man's word instead. They present studies defining their church, not God's. These teachings may masquerade under such titles as Primary Principles, Basic Beliefs, or Foundational Studies. While the titles sound good, all too often they are teachings about man's institutions, not the

Word of God. They are not Bible studies at all but lessons that use the Bible to try to validate a preconceived, human point of view.

If pressured by denominational hierarchy or sectarian Church leaders, false teachers will often ignore or defy the true Word of God and present error. They may not start out to deceive, but they soon find that if they want to keep their job they must do as they are told. They must teach what they are given to teach or be replaced.

FALSE TEACHERS ADD TO OR TAKE AWAY FROM THE WORD: Fourth, even if a false teacher knows the Word, he may mock it by adding to it or subtracting from it. To cover his ignorance or to deliberately mislead people into a particular belief or ministry, a false teacher will embellish God's Word. He may add or introduce doctrines or heresies that are not authenticated by holy Scripture (2 Peter 2:1).

In adding to the Word, he may insist that he or the ministry he serves has had special revelation that is not spoken of in God's Word but which is valid and must be shared in today's world. He may claim that an oral or a supernatural word or manifestation that he has received has as much or even more credibility than does the already whole Word of God.

He or his group may even pass out their own "bibles" which, they claim, further amplify God's Word or explain the "parts He left out." They will use these false bibles as their primary teaching source, and they often ingeniously point to or quote holy Scripture taken out of context to prove their deception.

Conversely, a false teacher may purposefully omit Scripture. He will claim much of it is irrelevant or not applicable today. This goes far beyond an unbalanced presentation of ministers of flesh, wherein certain parts of Scripture are so aggrandized that no time or room is left for other instruction. This is purposefully prohibiting the knowledge of certain parts of the Word or deliberately denying some of the Word. It is nullifying by omission God's stated will and ways.

It is not coincidence that the parts of the Bible most often withheld by a false teacher have to do with the portrait of unregenerate man as a sinful creature who needs to be reconciled with the Father. It is not coincidence that the parts of holy Scripture most often omitted speak of Jesus and His substitutionary, sacrificial death as the only way to the Father. It is not a coincidence that, after expunging the cross as the central Christian experience, false teachers introduce their own version of salvation, the doctrine of works rather than faith.

False teachers withhold information about the cross of Christ.

The ultimate purpose of adding to or subtracting from Scripture is to promote a particular cult or god. It is to lie to the unwary, falsely promising them new, easy truth. Whether by addition or omission, it deceives about the true teachings of Christ. In its worst form, it introduces new doctrines or whole new religions whose pillars are based on a lying, deceiving spirit (1 Timothy 4:1).

When false teachers of the new religions have entrapped their victims, they won't allow them to read the real Bible for fear they will find out the truth and leave the false fold. Ultimately, in adding to or subtracting from God's Word, false teachers mock God. They present totally unscrupulous, error-laden heresy.

FALSE TEACHERS LACK BALANCE: A fifth error in teaching concerns lack of balance. While a true teacher will present a many-sided, balanced instruction, a false teacher will not. Perhaps again because of denominational pressure or maybe for personal reasons, a false teacher can have tunnel vision. He teaches one thing to the almost total exclusion of others. He picks and chooses what he will teach, dwelling on it endlessly. In the process, he leaves out vital fields of study. He denies parts of the whole Word by ignoring them or refusing to refer to them.

False teachers lack balance in their choice of topics.

By locking himself and the Church into one area of study, a false teacher can both control a Church and keep it in a very immature state. If he erroneously and endlessly drones on concerning one subject, the Church is in bondage. This lack of balance will not show up in a week or even a month. It would be wise for every saint to look back on lessons received over a year's time. It would be wise to see if his local Church is in a rut or over-focused in one area. It would be well to question if one thing has been presented to the total exclusion of others. From there, it would be well to ascertain if the Church has become unbalanced or known for one particular teaching or belief rather than functioning in the whole balanced Word of God. Such is the fruit of false teachers.

FALSE TEACHERS CONFUSE THE ISSUES: Next, while a true teacher of God instructs in a simple, concise, clear manner, a false teacher will not. Rather than simple, he will teach complicated theories in a way-out jargon that no one can follow. Rather than concisely, he often bores people to death with long-winded nonsense. Rather than clearly, his lessons often leave his students with the feeling of having walked through muddy water.

On the other hand, a false teacher may copy or imitate good teaching methods. He can easily and even professionally present his lessons of error with a slickness that could deceive even the most discerning.

FALSE TEACHERS DON'T FOCUS ON JESUS: Finally, a true teacher focuses his teachings on the reality and beauty of Christ but a false teacher will not. Whether he instructs on feel-good topics, opines on things originating in himself (*John 7:28*) or presents doctrines that demons teach (*1 Timothy 4:1*), someone or something other than Jesus will predominate in his teachings. Since his goal is to bring attention to self or to his unholy master and his heresies, a false teacher will seldom, if ever, consistently focus on or present teachings concerning the Lord.

Thus the false teacher is the antithesis of the true one. Essentially he does not teach in a way that edifies or unites the Church (which is one of the purposes of the gift) but in a manner that tears down and divides the body. He is not a man of God.

THE FRUIT OF FALSE TEACHERS

The result of this ministry of madness is twofold. First, to the Church, the end products of false teaching are division, diversion, uproar, confusion, and error.

Second, to the false teachers themselves, the results are disastrous. God has warned in His Word that not many should become teachers because those who do assume a higher accountability *(James 3:1)*. Those who have not heeded that word and who have become false teachers are given further warnings. To the unrepentant, certain destruction is coming!

> ....*there were also false teachers among you, who will secretly bring in destructive heresies, even denying the Lord who bought them, and bring on themselves swift destruction.* 2 Peter 2:1 (NKJV)

> ....*for a long time their judgment has not been idle, and their destruction does not slumber.* 2 Peter 2:3 (NKJV)

God is very concerned when saint and sinner are being led astray. He has clearly warned all those involved in the deception. Because God has so often delayed His punishment does not mean that it is not forthcoming. He is extending His mercies to give the errant ones time to turn around and mend their ways. When His grace period is over, He will act. Heed the Word of the Lord!

OUR RESPONSE TO THE FALSE TEACHER

SEEK GOD: Finally, the saints must decide what they will do about all of this. None of us has led such a sheltered life that we have been immune from error. Therefore, we must ask God to show us the parts of our life that were brought into place by true, godly teaching and the parts of our walk that were effected by false teaching from a fleshly or an unholy spirit. In short, we must once more discern. We must learn if the place we've been led to and the teachings we hold dear are the product of the Holy Spirit or of a not so holy one. To help us do so, the Word says: *"We are of God. He who knows God hears us; he who is not of God does not hear us. By this we know the spirit of truth and the spirit of error"* (1 John 4:6 NKJV).

REPENT: Next, as we begin to identify areas in which we have willingly or ignorantly been led astray, we must repent. We must acknowledge and confess as sin the fact that false teachers have sinned against God *(Isaiah 43:27)*, against the body of Christ, and against individual believers. We must also confess our sin in allowing it to happen. Additionally, we must confess our sin if we have been one of those false teachers. After confessing these sins, we must ask forgiveness for them. Having been forgiven, we, in turn, must forgive.

WITHDRAW FROM THE FALSE: We dare not stop there. God's instructions about dealing with false teachers continue. We are charged to withdraw from false teachers and false teachings: *"From such withdraw yourself"* (1 Timothy 6:5 NKJV). Further, we must reject these counterfeit ones from Christian fellowship. *"Reject a divisive man after the first and second admonition"* (Titus 3:10 NKJV).

BE ON GUARD: After that, we must be on guard. After having cleaned our own temple and the house of God, we face one of the most severe tests. It is necessary to keep them clean. As 2 John 9-10 (NKJV) says:

> Whoever transgresses and does not abide in the doctrine of Christ does not have God. He who abides in the doctrine of Christ has both the Father and the Son. If anyone comes to you and does not bring this doctrine, do not receive him into your house nor greet him.

The important word in these verses is "anyone." It means we must put God above any other relationship.

Avoid those who teach doctrinal error. Anyone can include a dear friend or neighbor who insists on plying us with false doctrine. Anyone can be a boss who ties our employment to the condition that we listen to or participate in discussions of false gospels. Anyone can include our pastor or other Church leaders who come to us with the intention of presenting error or asking us to believe it and govern our lives by it. Most heart breaking of all, anyone can include members of our own family who insist on barraging us with doctrinal error, including parents, brothers, step-sisters, cousins, in-laws, and favorite uncles. In short, these people are not to be received, accepted, welcomed, or admitted into our homes if they bring false teaching and thus the doctrine of antichrist with them.

As a more positive instruction in combatting false teaching, we must herald and teach the Word. We must, *"Preach the Word! Be ready in season and out of season. Convince, rebuke, exhort, with all longsuffering and teaching"* (2 Timothy 4:2 NKJV).

The verses preceding this Scripture tell us that the Word is God's, that it is inspired, and that it was given, *"for instruction, reproof, correction, and training in righteousness"* (2 Timothy 3:16 NKJV). It further states that by the Word the man of God is complete, proficient, and equipped for every good word (2 Timothy 4:17).

It is a good work to refute false teaching. It is a good work to preach the Word. It is God's own planning that He has left to the Church the greatest weapon available for exposing error: the truth found in His Word. We are to be ready at any time to refute error and promote truth by using His own Word.

The question is: are we willing to do so?

TEACHERS

	THE TRUE	THE FALSE
CHARACTER:	have integrity	• lack integrity • base • proud • ignorant of the truth
PURPOSE:	• instruct those hungry for God • instruct on the basics of Christianity as found in the Word of God	• prey on the unwary • present denominational doctrines, traditions of men, sectarianism, and the letter of the law • introduce error
LEVELS:	**THE GRACE:** those who love to study the Word and gradually begin to teach it in the local Church **THE MINISTRY:** those whose ability to teach the Word expands to the local commnity **THE TEACHER:** those who have the authority and integrity to teach the Word of God at a worldwide level	• the immature who are given the authority to teach too quickly-- don't know the topic or how to present it so it does not bear fruit or change lives • present their own thoughts • speak in flesh • no anointing/ no fruit • self-promoting • demonically inspired • pawn of Satan
METHODS:	• lessons are clear, concise, systematic • present truth until it is learned and is being applied to life • teach balanced subject matter • progrssive • bring life • teach truth	• lessons are muddy, confusing, and have no planned order • present falsehoods that do not promote the kingdom of God • endlessly drill on one topic • stagnant • bring boredom, indifference, and death • present lies, hearsay, personal beliefs • flatter the ears of men • pander to the desires of people's hearts

FIRE

Several facts are evident from the reading of the Word:

1. The Lord has established on earth a body called the Church (*Matthew 16:18*). It is made up of born-again believers in God who, upon meeting together in one area, form a local assembly. The sum of the local assemblies worldwide is known as the universal Church.

2. Jesus not only laid the foundation for the Church but is also the foundation for the Church (*1 Corinthians 3:16*). Jesus is the Rock upon whom the whole Church is built and rests. No man and no false god can take this honor from Him.

3. The purpose for establishing the Church was to raise a people who would carry out His divine commission to preach the gospel to every creature, to make disciples of all nations, to deliver, and to heal (*Matthew 28:19-20; Mark 16:15-18*).

4. It was prophetically proclaimed by Jesus that power was to be a hallmark of His Church; the gates of hell would not prevail against it (*Matthew 16:18*).

5. God gave mankind a master plan for building the Church so that it could do what it was and is supposed to

do in power. Just as He gave Moses an exact and detailed strategy for building the tabernacle in Old Testament times, so now, in New Testament days, He left a blueprint for building His Church. It is found in His Word.

6. This plan to build the Church calls for the raising up and the functioning of apostles, prophets, evangelists, pastors, and teachers. Their job is to equip the saints for the work of ministry and to edify the body of Christ until its members come into a unity of faith, a knowledge of Jesus, and a maturity or a measure of the stature of the fullness of Christ *(Ephesians 4:11-13)*.

7. It is quite evident that this plan has not yet come to pass. The Church is not fully functioning in power, and the saints are not wholly equipped, edified, or matured to carry out the great commission. However, it is also quite evident that this program will come to pass. God has spoken it, and it is true whether it can yet be visibly seen or not.

God's Word does not lie. Even though God's design has not yet perfectly come to pass, that is no reason to believe that it will not. Delay is not denial or defeat. The actuality of an empowered Church, the emplacement of its leaders, and the accomplishment of God's will and words by the saints is happening. Therefore it is more important than ever that God's will be learned, accepted, and followed. It is more important than ever that His plan to raise the Church becomes and remains fully operational until these things are wholly accomplished.

There is, of course, a hindrance in the process. Satan is aware of all these facts and is doing his utmost to keep them from becoming reality. Although he understands that he cannot ultimately keep God's Word from coming to pass, he also realizes that many saints do not know that Word and that many others are not truly convinced of God's total authority and power. So, although working from a position of total defeat, Satan has deceived, distracted, and diverted many saints from keeping God's commands to build His Church and to function in it.

As a result, a counterfeit church system has arisen. While God has His true Church and is raising up its leaders who follow His Word, a counterfeit religious system has arisen which opposes both God's Church and His Word. The false church is a God-less, religious system of death. Its leaders are either ministers of flesh or the outright agents of Satan.

Out of the midst of the confusion that this is causing sounds the mighty Word of God:

> For no other foundation can anyone lay than that which is laid, which is Jesus Christ. Now if anyone builds on this foundation with gold, silver, precious stones, wood, hay, straw, each one's work will become clear; for the Day will declare it, because it will be revealed by fire; and the fire will test each one's work, of what sort it is. 1 Corinthians 3:11-13 (NKJV)

God is going to put both the true and the false to the test. It is to be a test of fire. By His decree: "If anyone's *work which he has built on it endures, he will receive a reward. If anyone's work is burned, he will suffer loss; but he himself will be saved, yet so as through fire"* (1 Corinthians 3:14-15 NKJV).

Each person and all of his or her work is to be tested. There are no exceptions! Those who have built upon the foundation of Christ with gold, silver, and precious stones will see their work submitted to the test of fire, endure the test, and receive a heavenly reward. Those who have piled wood, hay, and straw on the holy foundation have only added combustible building material that will burst into flame when the testing fire reaches them. These building materials may produce sparks for a while, but ultimately they will be reduced to ashes.

Fire has several purposes. For example, in industry fire is used to test or try something. It is used to purge impurity. It is used to strengthen and harden. Also, since fire consumes, it is used to burn waste.

Personally, fire can be a great blessing. On a cold day, it brings warmth; in a dark night, it lights the way. Or, in a time of distress, a warm, cheerful fire brings great comfort.

Holy fire serves these same purposes. God sends it to test and try saints. He turns up the fire to cleanse out impurity. He uses fire to strengthen, temper, and set His holy ones. Since God is a consuming fire *(Hebrews 12:29)*, He uses it to burn up the waste of our sins and our works of flesh.

In God's kingdom, fire from heaven can signal God's presence, approval, and power (1 Kings 18:36-39; Acts 2:1-4). When God made His covenant with Abram, He sent holy fire to sanctify it (Genesis 15:17). The Lord introduced Himself to Moses in a burning bush (Exodus 3:2). A pillar of fire led the Hebrew children in the wilderness (Exodus 40:38). Holy fire fell on the disciples who were gathered in the upper room (Acts 2:3), and the Church holds the promise that the Lord will return in flaming fire (2 Thessalonians 1:7-8).

One of the most exciting ways that God revealed Himself by fire was at the dedication of the priesthood that was to serve in the Tabernacle of Moses. When the work on the tabernacle had been finished, the glory of the Lord filled the place. So great was the cloud upon it and so wonderful was the glory within it that Moses was not able to enter the tabernacle (Exodus 40:33-35).

Soon after, at the consecration of the priests, the glory of the Lord again appeared (Leviticus 9:23). Then, in a mighty act of power, fire came out from before the Lord and consumed the offering and the fat on the altar. With no help from man, holy fire sovereignly ignited God's choice of worship (the sacrifice), His place of worship (the altar), and the hearts of those who were to serve Him (the priests). He intended that His holy fire would never go out (Leviticus 6:13).

By so doing, God established some principles of worship. First, the fire of sacrifice and worship was to be eternal. Second, God would approve of and accept only those offerings that were holy. Third, all worship offered to Him by priests had to be ignited by holy fire rather than by flesh or by the profane. Fourth, this supernatural act of God, the sending of holy fire, made Him the source of all true fire. Holy fire and holy fire alone was to be offered by priests in holy service. Any other fire offered to Him from any other source would therefore be strange or false fire.

However, even as He blessed His holy ones with holy fire in order to show His approval, God has also used fire to announce His disapproval. To some, fire proved to be awful, terrifying, and destructive. It was a judgment on the unholy *(Isaiah 4:4)*. The same fire that warms the house, lights its dark corners, and comforts us can also burn it down.

God has always separated Himself from the unclean or the profane. When unholy men offered unholy sacrifices using unholy fire from unholy sources, they were offering that which God could neither approve nor accept. Their sacrifices were nothing but show, fakery, pretense, or sham. They were blatant attempts to make people believe that God's blessing rested upon those people and those things that were not holy.

The same is true today. False fire is false worship offered by false leaders to false gods. False fire does not strengthen but weakens the deceived. It is not a part of true worship to holy God, but rather it is a part of a false system of worship to an unholy god. It is based on presumption, rebellion, and idolatry. It is a substitutionary ministry of flesh or of outright iniquity that, without question, has, is, and will come under judgment.

PRESUMPTION

The Old Testament gives us examples of three types of false worship by false fire: the false fires of presumption, rebellion, and idolatry. The book of Leviticus, chapter ten, tells us about God's judgment falling on false fire because of the sin of presumption.

Immediately after the glory of God had fallen at the dedication of the priests in the Tabernacle of Moses and fire had come from the midst of His presence to burn the sacrifices, the people of God fell on their faces in awe, fear, and the desire to worship (Leviticus 9:24). Not so Nadab and Abihu. They, not in worship but in presumption, grabbed their censers, put fire from an unholy source in them, added incense to them, and offered profane fire before the Lord (Leviticus 10:1). As a result of their iniquity, fire came out from God a second time and devoured them (Leviticus 10:2).

What had Nadab and Abihu done that was so awful? Wasn't it good to worship the Lord? Why then was such a drastic judgment meted out? The answers to these questions lie in who committed the offense, how they did it, and why it was done.

First, these men were sons of the high priest. Growing up in a home where awe, reverence, and obedience to God should have been the norm, they, more than any others, should have known not to do what they did. Because of their relationship with Aaron and because they were priests and leaders, their offense was more serious. God had to show His displeasure in a spectacular way so that others would not follow their example.

Second, concerning their methods, when fire came out from the presence of God and went to the brazen altar, holy fire from holy God made that altar a holy place. Other than in the tabernacle, God had not honored another place in the Hebrew camp with holy fire.

Ignoring all of this, Nadab and Abihu took fire from another source. While the people were on their faces before God in worship, these two got busy in flesh. They put false fire, fire of unholy origin, in their censers and offered an unholy offering. The false fire was not from holy God but from unholy man. Therefore, it was not an offering of true worship but of false worship. It was not done in God's way but in man's way. Since the source of their fire was man and not God, theirs was an offering of flesh. As a work of flesh, it showed supreme contempt for holiness. The Word labeled their offering profane (*Leviticus 10:1*).

Third, Nadab and Abihu acted in arrogance. They did that which God had not commanded them to do and then had the effrontery to offer the abomination to holy God. They had been given no instruction from God to do such a thing, but they did it anyway. They were not acting in obedience but in overfamiliarity with holy things. In a response of presumption rather than of faith, they did what they chose to do in the way they chose to do it. Since they violated God's command in what they did and how they did it, they were judged by fire.

After their deaths, God spoke to His people through Moses and warned them against any further lack of holiness: *"And Moses said to Aaron, 'This is what the LORD spoke, saying: "By those who come near Me I must be regarded as holy; and before all the people I must be glorified" ' "* (Leviticus 10:3 NKJV).

He also commanded the priests to learn to distinguish between the holy and the unholy, the clean and the unclean. As Leviticus 10:9-10 (NKJV) says:

> Do not drink wine or intoxicating drink, you, nor your sons with you, when you go into the tabernacle of meeting, lest you die. It shall be a statute forever throughout your generations, that you may distinguish between holy and unholy, and between unclean and clean.

The application of lessons learned in this situation are plentiful to the Church. Are there Nadabs and Abihus in the Church today? Are there those who minister unto holy God in an unholy way or those who minister in a holy place in a profane way? Are those who have received no direction from God doing what seems good to them to do and then offering the iniquity to holy God? This is the essence of false worship and false religion.

Ministering by false fire teaches disrespect for the commands of God. It gives credence to a ministry of flesh or in-church humanism. It raises man's will over God's and gives man's ways authority in worship and service. It says that man can determine how he will worship God. We hear the echo of this presumption in the New Testament Church:

> Not everyone who ways to Me, "Lord, Lord" shall enter the kingdom of heaven, but he who does the will of My Father in heaven. Many will say to Me in that day, "Lord, Lord, have we not prophesied in Your name, cast out demons in Your name, and done many wonders in Your name?" And then I will declare to them, "I never knew you; depart from Me, you who practice lawlessness!" Matthew 7:21-23 (NKJV)

God has clearly warned that we must not engage in presumption or unholy activity of the flesh. Those who offer false fire will not, in the long run, be able to stand before God. Offenders in false fire will be judged and dealt with. They will be overcome and destroyed by the very thing they profaned—true, holy fire.

> For behold, the LORD will come with fire and with His chariots, like a whirlwind, to render His anger with fury, and His rebuke with flames of fire. For by fire and by His sword the LORD will judge all flesh; and the slain of the LORD shall be many. Isaiah 66:15-16 (NKJV)

As a final thought concerning the false fire of presumption, God has also commanded His saints to learn to distinguish between the holy and the unholy, the clean and the unclean. Discerning as to whether or not worship, service, and ministry unto holy God is true or false lies squarely on the shoulders of His priests—today's believers (Leviticus 10:10).

REBELLION

There is another prominent example of offering false fire to God in the Old Testament. The sixteenth chapter of the book of Numbers records the story of false fire whose source was rebellion.

Korah, Dathan, and Abiram were important men. They were leaders in Israel. Korah was of the Levitical line of Kohath (Numbers 16:1), and Dathan and Abiram were among the chief descendants of Reuben. Rather than instantly and presumptuously offering false fire to God, these men were involved in a carefully planned defiance of God. Worse yet, they had influenced 250 other chiefs and leaders to join them in their conspiracy and rebellion against the leadership which God had placed over them.

Publicly confronting Moses and Aaron, they pressed their charges against God's anointed. They claimed that Moses and Aaron took too much on themselves, that the whole congregation of Israel and not just these two leaders was holy, and that Moses and Aaron were exalting themselves (Numbers 16:3).

None of these accusations were valid. Moses and Aaron had not taken on too much; the whole congregation was not holy (as the conspirators themselves were proving even at that moment); and God had raised the brothers into leadership *(Exodus 3:10; 4:14-16; Leviticus 9:23)*. In truth, the complaints were merely words of unholy, proud, ambitious men who were jealous of the men who God had placed as leaders over the nation and over the priesthood.

The real issue was that the rebellion was not against men, but against God. What a great blessing it was that Moses discerned the situation and did not compromise his calling. There was no doubt in his mind as to who he was and Who had placed him in that position. His questioned leadership quickly sprang forth. Rather than defending himself, he wisely announced that God would judge the matter *(Numbers 16:5)*.

Then, he laid out the rules by which the challenge would be met. There was to be a test of fire. The mutineers were to put fire and incense in their censers and burn them before the Lord. Aaron was to do the same with his censer. The one whom the Lord chose would be proclaimed as holy *(Numbers 16:7)*.

Time was given for the defiant ones to repent. Instead, the rebellion and accusations grew worse *(Numbers 16:12-14)*. Rather than confessing their sin and submitting to authority, the unholy ones pressed on in their disobedience.

The next day at the agreed upon time, the challengers and the challenged met. Joining them was the glory of the Lord *(Numbers 16:19)*. The same glory that fell to install Aaron as priest now fell to publicly confirm him in that office.

However, judgment also fell. God destroyed those acting in flesh. The ground opened up and swallowed the leaders of the rebellion *(Numbers 16:31-32)*. Then, consuming fire came forth from the Lord and devoured the 250 men who had offered false fire.

An interesting sidelight of the whole incident is that Eleazar the priest then took the censers of the rebellious ones and pounded them into metallic sheets for a covering for the altar of sacrifice *(Numbers 16:39)*. The censers were made of bronze. Bronze symbolizes judgment. These men, through rebellion, had brought judgment on themselves.

Again, this offering of false fire can be seen in the twenty-first century Church. Some in today's Church are like Korah, greedy for what they do not have and jealous of those who have it. They are willing to do anything to get what they want. Also, there are those like Korah who have falsely raised themselves into leadership positions, proclaimed their own calling, and then tried to drive out, suppress, or prevent those truly chosen by God from occupying and serving in their anointed positions. The holy are still being challenged by the unholy.

Two thousand years ago, Jesus proclaimed His Church. It was to be a submitted body that would work to extend His kingdom. In order to be a governed body, the Lord had to raise up leaders who would listen to Him and obey Him. Quite simply, if Jesus was to be the Head of His Church, then the leadership (those who represented Him to the body) had to be His chosen ones.

That same principle should apply to today's Church. All too often, it does not. When flesh aspires to or unlawfully arises to leadership, the war is on. It is often fought on two battlefronts.

First, it is not uncommon to see God-ordained leadership being challenged by twenty-first century Korahs. Those with false claims to leadership, full of greed and self-importance, put false fire in their censers and defy God's anointed. Second, there are those who already occupy illegally assumed positions of leadership within the Church and don't want to give them up. Suspicious and fearful, rather than serving God, they spent too much of their time trying to squeeze out, suppress, or enslave all those they consider a threat to their unholy throne.

THE FIRST BATTLEGROUND—THE REBELLIOUS CHALLENGE GOD'S LEADERS: If God's chosen leaders walk in their anointed positions of leadership and do as God commands them to do, they often become targets. Leadership doesn't mean letting people go where they want to go or allowing them to do only what is right in their own eyes. It means leading them in the ways of God and overseeing them as they learn submission to His will. It means discipline, love, justice, compassion, holiness, and mercy.

Some who refuse to be governed or comforted rebel. False leaders will not submit to God's leadership and often break away from God's chosen plan. They then encourage others to do the same. They begin to see themselves as supervisors popularly leading the people in the way they want to go. Then, with unholy visions of grandeur, they try to bring those rebelling with them under their own, not God's, authority. The one thing that stands in the way of their taking over the Church and ruling it for and by themselves is the rightful anointed leadership that God placed over them. Therefore, in their view, the holy leaders must be gotten out of the way.

Pride and ambition are not the only motives of the unholy in challenging the holy. Greed plays an important part too.

The unscrupulous know a good thing when they see it. They see some Church leaders living like kings. Some leaders are given houses. Often their bills are paid. They command attention. To some, it seems that they endlessly sleep late, have lunch with the boys, and have afternoons free for golf. In return, little or nothing seems to be required of them.

Looks can be deceiving. A true man of God in no way relates to the above lifestyle.

Like Korah and company, the unholy challenge the holy with no regard at all for God's appointment or His anointing. They conspire against and raise themselves up against true leaders. Also, like Korah and friends, the accusers of true leadership are often influential men. Differences are not so much in position as they are in character.

The challenge is between the submitted and the rebellious, the holy and the unholy, regardless of station in life. It is long past time for God's true body to understand that those who see themselves, raise themselves, and pronounce themselves as holy are often none of the above.

A second problem is that the unholy keep those who are truly anointed to serve out of leadership positions. Some pastors, especially those who control local Churches and run one-man shows, cannot bear the thought of sharing the glory—or the finances—of leadership with anyone. They want things done their way in "their" Church. Not acknowledging God's right to raise leaders, false leaders assume this authority for themselves and put people in positions in their Church who think as they do, do as they are told, and present no threat to their false leader's dictatorship.

However, much to their chagrin, God is greater than manipulation and domination. He has the annoying habit (to some people's way of thinking) of choosing, calling, equipping, and spotlighting His choice of leaders. He anoints them with holy fire and His light on them cannot be hidden or denied. All they say and do is an expression of their submission to and their love for holy God. As they grow in the Lord, others see the light of God in them long before they see it in themselves, and they begin to respond to it.

The presence of His light makes the false leader's darkness darker. Holiness makes lack of holiness very obvious. Holiness upsets man's plans and traditions. It brings life. It presents a different order, a contrast, a longing for something better, a separation from the profane. It causes people to see that there is a better way, God's way, which has been hidden and smothered in endless works of flesh.

False leaders are thoroughly frightened by the sight of God raising up a leader after His own kind. They are terrified at the reality of the Spirit of God resting upon someone in their congregation. False leaders know that if saints see a true anointing of God functioning in the house of God, they are going to ask for more of it. They are going to demand that which false leaders cannot supply.

No longer will there be contentment with or acceptance of the mediocre, boring, or counterfeit. Those never chosen by God to serve, in fear for their kingdoms and the good life, will do all they can to squelch and suppress the truly chosen. Thus, in a different way, the holy are again being challenged by the unholy.

Such evil pretenders to leadership in the house of God have not learned that a weapon formed against God's anointed will not prosper. It will simply bring judgment on the one who used it.

After doing all of this, many defiant ones turn around, smile at God, fill their censers full of false fire, and raise them to God. In holding up their brazen censers they bring judgment upon themselves. They don't know that they have done just as Korah, Datham, and Abiram did.

They've challenged those God raised to leadership and claimed an anointing they did not have. Further, in many cases, they brought a company of people against the holy to try, by the force of numbers, to get them to abdicate the positions that God gave them so that they could take over.

Such tactics didn't work thousands of years ago and they will not work today. God is raising up servants like Moses and Aaron who know they have God-given authority. He's calling to those who will let Him judge good and evil. He's strengthening those who will challenge the enemy's lie. He's ordaining those who will go on with His holy business even in the midst of turmoil and even while the fire of judgment falls on fools.

Everyone should know that there is but one true God. The Bible declares Him to be the God of the spirits of all flesh (*Numbers 16:22*). His fire is far more powerful than the pitiful flames of the rebellious. His holy, consuming fire rejects all false fire. Those who are today's Korahs are warned—their end is disaster!

> *Woe to them! For they have gone in the way of Cain, have run greedily in the error of Balaam for profit, and perished in the rebellion of Korah. These are spots in your love feasts, while they feast with you without fear, serving only themselves. They are clouds without water, carried about by the winds; late autumn trees without fruit, twice dead, pulled up by the roots; raging waves of the sea, foaming*

up their own shame; wandering stars for whom is reserved the blackness of darkness forever. Jude 11-13 (NKJV)

THE SECOND BATTLEFIELD—THE REBELLIOUS CHALLENGE FALSE LEADERS: Although there are many instances when the rebellious challenge holy leadership in the church, there are also instances when the rebellious challenge false leadership.

Some false challengers to Church government wrongfully occupy positions and titles that were never given to them by God, and they do works He never commanded them to do. They are those who have been raised by self, man, or the enemy. They occupy places not rightfully theirs and minister in the flesh. Long-entrenched in their illegal positions, they will not give them up. The positions where these false leaders have implanted or intertwined themselves hold the Church in bondage to flesh and to evil. False leaders perhaps believe that being in a holy place will make them holy and therefore acceptable to God and man. They do not understand that their unlawful presence simply contaminates and makes profane the altars at which they serve.

The immediate fruit of such an unholy state is trouble. It is fighting among men and ministries. It is a clash of flesh within the Church.

The false leaders are challenged other false leaders. False leaders from various local churches suspiciously eye one another, spot weaknesses, and move in for the kill.

False leaders are jealous of one another's flocks, buildings, and callings. Instead of cooperating to extend the kingdom of God, they compete to extend their own empires and diminish those of others. If other false leaders won't follow them and fall under their control, they shut them out, promote sectarianism, and command their followers not to fellowship with "those others who don't think like we do."

No one really wins in this squabbling. The saints, in desperate need of holy, godly leadership, definitely lose. Even worse, the light of false fires keeps God's holy fire out of the true Church.

IDOLATRY

Just as presumption and rebellion lead many to offer false fire, so does the sin of idolatry. As Scripture proves, God will not be mocked. He will not accept false fire. He will neither receive false worship nor acknowledge false leaders. Nor will He allow the fires of idolatry to burn.

Elijah was one who clearly understood God's mastery of fire and the effect that holy fire had on the unholy idols of men. He therefore used fire to challenge the system of idolatry that so enslaved Israel.

Baal was the god of the Canaanites, and was likened to Jupiter and the sun. He had been introduced to the Israelites by the goddess of witchcraft, Jezebel (1Kings 16:31-32). Baal was a god of fertility whose religious rites were orgies of unparalleled cruelty (slaughter of children) and perversion (licentiousness and prostitution). His minions burned incense to Him (Jeremiah 7:9) and burned their sons as offerings to Him (Jeremiah 19:5). Both of these evil deeds required the use of fire. One source, *The Pilgrim Bible Study*, states that Baal was the god of fire.

It was in this stronghold of idolatry and the worship of false gods that Elijah contested for God. It was against fire, the area of enemy strength, that the battle was enjoined. It was here by a test of fire that Elijah challenged false gods and their false fire of idolatry and won. First Kings chapter eighteen tells the story.

Elijah was incensed that God's people were serving another god. He cried out to them, rebuked them, and asked how long they world falter between two opinions (*1 Kings 18:21*). When the people wouldn't respond, he threw down the gauntlet. To show the utter impotence of Baal and the wickedness and offense that worshipping him was to God, Elijah challenged the idol's power.

Elijah commanded that two bulls be brought to be offered as sacrifices. The 450 prophets of Baal were to offer one bull, and he, the prophet of God, would offer the other.

To complete a sacrifice, the animals had to be burned. That required fire. Elijah issued the challenge that neither Baal's unholy minions nor he could light or apply fire to the sacrificial offerings (*1 Kings 18:23*). It was agreed that Baal's servants would call out to their god and that Elijah would call out to Jehovah. The God who answered by fire was to be acknowledged by all as the powerful, true God (*1 Kings 18:24*).

Baal's prophets went first. They chose a bull, prepared it, and called on their god to show his power by sending fire to kindle the sacrifice. There was no response.

Again, they tried communicating with their god. They called out and leaped around the altar they had made. For several hours they shouted even louder while Elijah mocked them. Not hearing from their god, they then became violent. They resorted to slashing their bodies with knives, a practice contrary to the command of God against gashing themselves (*Deuteronomy 14:1*). In essence, they offered their god the sacrifice of their own blood (*1 Kings 18:26-29*).

The result: no one answered; no one paid attention (*1 Kings 18:29*).

Then it was Elijah's turn. First, he repaired an old altar where the Lord had once been honored (*1 Kings 18:30*). He dug a trench, prepared the wood, cut up the bull, and laid it out. Then, three times he called for water, a fire-prohibiting agent, to be poured over the sacrifice and the wood.

In direct contrast to the practices of the false prophets, quietly, humbly, he sought God. Living his faith, he announced that God was the God of Israel and that he, Elijah, was His servant (*1 Kings 18:37*). He asked God to move, to manifest Himself not so that Elijah would be glorified but so that people would know the same truth that Elijah did: that Jehovah, and He only, was God.

Elijah's fiery zeal for God ended in a fiery demonstration of power from God. As soon as the words were out of Elijah's mouth, fire fell and consumed the offering, the wood, the stones, the dust, and even the water in the trench (*1 Kings 18:38*). That was holy fire!

The results were twofold: the people fell on their faces and acknowledged that Jehovah was God, and the false ministers were slain.

The lessons to be learned from all of this are obvious. First, there are yet Jezebels who openly challenge the leadership that God has ordained in his Church. There are false ministers and counterfeit ministries within the Church whose goals are to introduce and honor false gods.

Second, although evil ministers and leaders abound and at times seem to grossly outnumber the true servants of God, there is yet a remnant in the true Church that serves in zeal, purity, and holiness. These are modern-day Elijahs who seek to live in and to work in holiness while they separate themselves from and destroy that which is unholy. To these, God will yet openly and publicly manifest His fire and His power.

Third, while the counterfeit church is busy erecting new altars and introducing new religions and new gods, the true Church of God, in spite of all attempts to keep it from doing so, is rebuilding the altar where once God was served. It is once more serving God in a place that once was holy; it is honoring the faith of its forefathers with a new holiness and consecration. This restored altar of the saints is the place where the redeemed and reconciled, the righteous and sanctified, the pure and holy meet God. It is a place where overcomers call out for the presence of holy, undefeated, totally victorious God.

Fourth, the holy remnant is preparing sacrifices on their altar. These are offerings of contrite and repentant hearts and the sacrifices of praise and worship. By calling out to God in a proper expression of worship by singing, shouting, and dancing as commanded to do in Scripture, saints are seeing holy fire fall. Requiring no rites of flesh, no idolatry, no screaming or self-abuse, with no imitation of dervishes and their insane frenzies of activity, God is honoring the simple request that He move in such a way that all will know He is God.

Fifth, when directly challenged by unholy, false gods, the Lord reigns supreme. The power of the enemy has been broken, and the power and glory of true God is becoming more manifest. In-church humanism, evil works, and demonic power can challenge Him, but they are no challenge to Him. No works of flesh or distortions of the demonic will force the Lord to respond or to send the holy fire of approval to the unholy, to recognize a false leader, or to bow before false gods. He cannot be defeated, and He will not honor the unholy. He is God!

Sixth, at last saints are learning that unholy fires and unholy altars breed deception. They're learning not to judge by their natural senses. False fire looks like real fire—it is the same in appearance and color. False fire even feels like real fire—it is hot. However, it is different in source.

So often in the past, saints have tested the things around them by natural rather than spiritual means. Therefore they have evaluated things on the basis of the fruit rather than the root. They have not discerned the source of the manifestation they are experiencing.

For example, saints hear of healing ministries and flock to the healer whether his power is from God or not. Further, they don't test those calling themselves apostles to determine what foundation they are laying and building on. They hear prophecy and act on it without ascertaining the spirit behind it. They respond to evangelists without discerning if he is leading them to a strange god. They submit to pastors without determining whether God has called them to those positions or whether there is any godly anointing on their lives. They allow themselves to be taught without ensuring that the source of the teaching or the spirit of the teaching glorifies God.

Now, however, the pendulum is beginning to swing in the opposite direction. Fire is being used to purge impurity. A remnant is allowing fire to cleanse them and their ministries. They are longing to come into such holiness and such worship that the fire of God will fall.

Seventh, all ministers of false gods will be destroyed. God will not be mocked. God has promised that for the unrepentant, the final end is the lake of fire. The fire which was used to injure and deceive will become the agent of judgment: *"But the cowardly, unbelieving, abominable, murderers, sexually immoral, sorcerers, idolaters, and all liars shall have their part in the lake which burns with fire and brimstone, which is the second death"* (Revelations 21:8 NKJV).

In the Bible there are numerous incidents where holy fire fell. There is no reason to believe that it cannot or will not do so again. The holy fire of approval will fall only on the holy. The holy fire of judgment will fall on the foolish.

It must always be remembered that once there were two altars, two bulls, two sacrifices offered, two deities called out to, two ministries represented, two methods of worship displayed, and two prayers offered. However, only one God answered, and He accepted only one of the ministers and only one of the sacrifices. His fire of approval fell only on the holy.

God does not or want need false fire and false leadership to fulfill His Word. His Word will be fulfilled without the "help" of flesh or the hindrance of evil.

WHY DOES GOD GRANT TIME?

God is using fire to test and to strengthen His saints. In His mercy, He is also granting offenders time to repent. Some will do so. They will change their minds, hearts, and actions, repair His altar, make ready a proper sacrifice, minister to God in holiness, and call upon the Lord to reveal Himself to them. As they wait on Him, holy fire will fall.

On the other hand, some will not repent. In spite of all warnings they have received, they will continue to practice evil. They will offer false worship, promote false leadership, and honor false gods. They will offer no true sacrifice or fire to God but expect Him to honor their false one. They will not wait on God but continue on in their works of flesh. They will see true fire fall on them—only to be consumed by it.

Saints can be assured that fire is going to fall. Whether to show approval or judgment, fire is going to fall. The same fire called for by Elijah long ago is being called for today by cleansed, earnest saints. As God honored His prophet's zeal years ago, so He will honor it now.

Though to some it is unnoticeable, the Church is in the biggest move of God it has ever known. As it happened before in the time of Zerubbabel, Ezra, and Nehemiah, there will be a three-part restoration of saints coming out of Babylon, a place of idolatry, and returning to God. God is separating out a remnant of those who will truly worship him. Already He has sent out the first wave of saints to oversee the restoration of the Church. The altar which truly honors God is being rebuilt, and with it, the house of God is being rebuilt. Following immediately will be a resurgence of truly priestly ministries. Those who will bring saints into repentance, into praise and worship, and into sanctification and consecration unto God will receive His blessing. Finally, walls will be rebuilt so that saints can dwell in unity and safety as they are governed by holy leadership. God will send to His saints those who will establish and keep order while ministry unto Him goes on.

God would exhort His struggling people:

Remnant, arise!

Wake from your slumber!

Come out of exile and join your true brothers and sisters!

Be about your Father's business.

Cast off the bondage of death.

Cast off the slavery of sin.

Cast off the chains of false worship.

Cast off the chains of false leadership.

Cast off the chains of idolatry.

Cast off the chains of false religious systems.

Seek Jesus for forgiveness of these sins.

Seek Jesus for deliverance from the power of these sins.

Yield to the Holy Spirit for separation from the past.

Yield to the Holy Spirit for consecration into the service of the King.

Return to God and build His altar and His house.

Return to God and restore His people.

Enter into praise and worship and renew your covenant with Him.

Return to God and function under proper leadership. Learn that such submission is one of the Church's strongest defenses.

God will judge the unholy, those who offer false fire to Him. He will burn their works of wood, hay, and straw. He will judge their presumption, rebellion, and idolatry.

On the other hand, God will honor the holy, those who offer holy fire to Him. He will accept their works of gold, silver, and precious stones. He will delight in their humility, obedience, and reverence. He will empower them to do His true works with true fire on earth as they are done in heaven.

Never, never doubt it! Fire will fall! Whether in judgment or in approval, holy fire will fall!

And the choice of how it falls, dear saints, is up to us.

www.ingramcontent.com/pod-product-compliance
Lightning Source LLC
Chambersburg PA
CBHW022003090426
42741CB00007B/869